SHORTCUTS

You cannot bypass God's process to realizing your potential. In SHORTCUTS, my friend Bob Hasson shares how progress is progressive—often occurring in stages and phases, little by little. This message will help you find meaning in the mundane, peace under pressure, and purpose in your pain.

JOHN BEVERE

Best-selling author and minister

Co-founder of Messenger International and MessengerX

In his book SHORTCUTS, Bob Hasson breaks apart the subjects of passion, our design, planning, and success in a way that only a father who has been there before and has developed a voice for it can do. The reality is that we are not going to get a different result if we don›t have a different process and tools that set us apart.

Get SHORTCUTS for everyone in your life. I know I will. It is a gift that will save them years of hard process and help them to walk out their journey with the confidence that God intended.

SHAWN BOLZ

TV host, podcaster, minister, best-selling author

www.bolzministries.com

This book is a must-read for anyone wanting to have lasting and long-term success in their life and dreams. These timeless truths come with experience, authority, and success forged through making mistakes, learning through them, and no SHORTCUTS.

If I could go back and give my 20-year-old self advice for life and leadership, I would tell myself to read SHORTCUTS. The message that this book brings is crucial for long-term success in a world that celebrates hurry, instant gratification, and cutting corners. Bob Hasson is someone who has impacted my life significantly as a friend, mentor, and someone I respect deeply, and what he writes in this book is connected to decades of real-life experience and years of conversations.

ZACK CURRY

Lead pastor, Jesus Culture San Diego

In Bob's new book, ~~SHORTCUTS~~, you will discover a pathway to clarity in your own pursuit of passion, purpose, and the people with whom you choose to surround yourself. As you read these significant truths, you will gain a journey that Bob has lived out in his daily choices of relational integrity, serving others with high levels of excellence, regardless of the personal cost. It is worth the cost, and Bob will show you the way!

LAUREN HASSON

Founder and director of Lifestreams Ministries

There are voices in every generation that God raises up who bring a message we need to hear, a message that calls us to a higher standard and equips us to thrive in the unique call God has on each of us. Bob Hasson, in his book ~~SHORTCUTS~~, writes not just as a successful businessman, but as a pastor and prophet with a passion to see people fulfill their God-given potential. This is a message that will both inspire and challenge you in the best of ways. If you are hungry to grow and be equipped in your purpose, this book is a must-read.

BANNING LIEBSCHER

Founder and pastor of Jesus Culture
Author of *Three Mile Walk: The Courage You Need to
Live the Life God Wants for You*

If you need to get "unstuck," this book will undoubtedly inspire you and give you the motivation needed for change, and it will help you on your journey of living a life of great significance! My life has been greatly enriched because of the ~~SHORTCUTS~~ message and my friendship with

Bob! ~~SHORTCUTS~~ will give you invaluable wisdom that only comes with the experience gained through years of hard work and sacrifice!

CHRIS QUILALA

Singer/songwriter and founding member of Jesus Culture

I loved reading this book! ~~SHORTCUTS~~ is both timely and pertinent to anyone wanting a compass to guide them through the storms of life and career. It is also a map for navigating passions, priorities, and work ethic. Bob Hasson does a wonderful job showing us what is possible if we dig deep, stay focused, and surround ourselves with the right inputs. I highly recommend ~~SHORTCUTS~~ to anyone interested in being an effective dreamer, visionary, or practical strategist.

DANNY SILK

President of Loving on Purpose

Bob Hasson's new book, ~~SHORTCUTS~~, is a thought-provoking and honest work for anyone seeking purpose, passion, and perseverance. In these pages, Bob distills his wealth of experience into practical knowledge and fatherly wisdom that is sure to challenge you while also giving you keys to steward your calling. I highly recommend this book to anyone who is ready to move forward in their career and calling with confidence, clarity, and courage.

KRIS VALLOTTON

Leader, Bethel Church, Redding, CA
Co-founder of Bethel School of Supernatural Ministry
Author of 13 books, including *The Supernatural Ways of Royalty*,
Heavy Rain and *Spiritual Intelligence*

FOREWORD BY **DARREN ROUANZOIN**

~~SHORT~~CUTS

**THE PROVEN PATH
TO PURPOSE, EXCELLENCE,
AND CALLING.**

BOB HASSON

Cover Design by Ian Royal Nelson processcreative.co

Interior Design by Printopya LLC printopya.com

Published by NEWTYPE Publishing

Paperback ISBN: 978-1-952421-21-1

eISBN: 978-1-952421-22-8

First Edition

Printed in the United States.

Lauren—You are the wisest person I know. Your love of God transmits through you to everyone you touch. You are my shining light and I love how you fiercely love me and our family. Thank you for our 34 years of marriage and always believing the best in me. I love you more than you could ever know.

David and Natthanit, Kyler and Perla, Isabella, and Sophia—It is such a joy to be your dad and to watch you all grow into such amazing human beings. I am so excited to see all that God has for your favor-filled lives.

Table of Contents

Acknowledgments

I want to thank Danny and Sheri Silk—All of this wild ride started with our friendship and your belief in me. We have walked through life together sharing our deepest fears and greatest joys. We have fallen in love with each other's families and become family. Was there ever a time when we did not know each other? It seems that way.

Shawn Bolz and Cherie Bolz—Every once in a while God gives a sacred gift, and you two have stolen our hearts. Our relationship is multifaceted and so fresh. Thank you both for trusting me and for launching me into areas that I never knew were possible. I am not sure I can take another one of your ideas!!!

Allison Armerding—Thanks again for all your effort and taking this project from conception to a beautiful finished product. Your ability to understand and portray my thoughts is amazing. I love working with you and recommend you to any aspiring writer. www.allisonarmerding.com

Jeremy and Dr. Ally Butrous—Wow, you two! From a fledgling idea to a beautiful book, thank you for all your help in every area of my life. You have the vision to see what the next steps are and how to direct me there with God's heart.

Thank you to Ryan Sprenger and the NEWTYPE Publishing team—Your planning, organization, and execution are amazing.

To the Greystone Crew—Something was established in all our hearts. Thank you all for being my closest friends and confidants. I love that you all know each other and am looking forward to more iron sharpening iron and fun adventures.

To our JCSD church family—We are so humbled and excited about what God is doing through this church plant. We love all the staff, hosts, and new family that is being created.

In my life, having someone call me friend is the greatest compliment. I am blessed to have a group of dear friends—you know who you are—and I want to recognize that each of you has deposited such love, richness, fun, and wisdom in my life. I am awed with how you conduct yourselves, live your lives, and battle for your faith, the relationships in your families, your friends, and your businesses. Thank you!

Foreword

Several years ago one of my mentors, Don Williams, an eighty-year-old pastor and theologian, introduced me to Bob Hasson. The morning turned to lunch time and then in the late afternoon Don grabbed both of our hands and said, "You need to be in each other's lives." Because, as Don says, "the meaning of life is relationships."

As you will read later in this book, "A counselor who has the ability to help you grow in wisdom is someone who has built their life on trust in God, has developed the traits of resilience––acceptance of reality, belief in meaning and purpose, and the ability to improvise––and has good fruit in their life to show for it." Bob has been a counselor to me and hundreds if not thousands of people, but most of all he has been my friend. He's a companion who's further along on the journey and with the passion and commitment to keep me grounded and moving forward. He has become a father to me as well as to my marriage, my family, my leadership, my church, and my life; and all of those are better because of my relationship with this man. He's the real deal: a man of integrity, character, insight, wisdom, love, and great joy. If you are like me, you probably feel a bit out of place at times, uncertain about where things are going or how to get to where you want to be. You might even be tempted to take a shortcut and arrive there without doing the hard work that's required. If you are searching for a way to get there, Bob Hasson has written a handbook for the coming generations to find their way. One might say it's prophetic and geared toward the future or that it's simply taking old truths and applying it to our current culture. Both are needed in this current crisis we are living in.

The crises of hurry, quick fixes, distractions, and unprocessed ~~SHORTCUTS~~ leave people feeling hurt, disoriented, disillusioned, and stuck. So many of us continue to walk down roads that lead us back to where we started. Many of us are stuck. We are stuck in the same habits and patterns that leave us longing for more and waiting for something to change. Many of us have turned to the wrong sources for the power to change. In the age of information, wisdom is a sacred and precious resource that, like the Proverbs writer says, "stands at the gates of the city." Wisdom is available for those who seek it, those who pursue it, and those who set aside cultural approaches to life and learn the way of life.

Bob gives you a roadmap on how to reconstruct your life and find true and tested ways of building a meaningful life. Within these pages you will not only take practical steps to get you to rethink your approach to work-life balance, passion, stewardship, and so on, but also discover ways of making decisions with discernment. You will discover how to find your purpose and reignite your passion, all from a biblical worldview. Bob will help you discover a mindset that realigns your life to sacred truths of old. He guides us to the crossroads and invites us to live a life of wisdom, rather than hurried reactions like the culture around us.

I am struck by the stunning wisdom of this book and the depth one can pull from each chapter. "We were designed to take things in chaos and bring them into order, to see problems and create solutions, to take things that are out of balance and bring them into balance." "We who are learning to build everything in our lives on a posture of trust have the potential to become--and should become--the most resilient people on the planet." "There are no SHORTCUTS to this amazing life--not because it's supposed to be hard, but because God doesn't want us to miss one moment of the journey!" Wisdom, perhaps, is not something one is born with. It's something one builds into their life over time. Bob has not taken SHORTCUTS. He has chosen to live his life based on the principles given in this book. Wisdom never comes without cost. Wisdom must be practiced, fought for, and lived. Wisdom is about mastering the art of living, and Bob has a fruitful life. He knows both the struggles and the ease, the pains and the pleasures, the grief and the joy. He has embodied the message within this work that reveals the greatest testimony to his message.

So, in these pages live not only an invitation but a handbook to pattern your life in a way that leads to that which is really life (see 1 Timothy 6:19). So, don't hurry and don't look for the easy road. Instead, open your heart, and go to work to build something good and beautiful. Build a life worth living.

Darren Rouanzoin
Lead Pastor Garden Church
Long Beach, CA

Introduction

Thank you for picking up this book. My heart is that within these pages you will find stories and truth that will help set you free in areas where you feel stuck or uncertain in your life and that will fill you with fresh courage and vision to move ahead on your path.

I have encountered those difficult places often in my own journey, and I am so grateful for the truth that has found and freed me as I have sought, and continue to seek, the path of both struggle and blessing in learning to trust God. Though I'm still in process, I want to share what I've learned with anyone who is on the same quest.

In 2017, I made my first real career pivot. I had spent nearly forty years building a business. Then, without really knowing what I was getting into, I took up the invitation of my friend Danny Silk, co-authored *The Business of Honor* with him, and ventured into the world of writing, speaking, and consulting. In 2019, my friend Shawn Bolz invited me into his world, and a year later we wrote *Wired to Hear* together and began a podcast, *Exploring the Marketplace*.

These men and my wife, Lauren, all saw something in me I did not see. Have you ever had someone believe the best in you, or see the destiny and favor God has on your life? Think back to words spoken over you, people who have given you courage, relationships that have made you a better human. We all need vital relationships to help us navigate this life and grow into the fullness of who God created us to be.

There are many things I could say about the roller coaster I have been on since I stepped out of my comfort zone as "the painter" and began learning how to be "Bob, the author, consultant, speaker, and podcaster." But the most important aspect of this new season and adventure has been the people.

Over the last five years, I have had hundreds of conversations with people in all stages of their careers and life. Typically, they want to talk to me about their job or business, but inevitably the conversation ends up touching the deeper matters of the heart—identity, purpose, and connection with God and others. Though they all have unique situations and circumstances, what has emerged over and over again are very similar struggles rooted in similar core issues—issues I know well because I have struggled with them myself.

Some people are frustrated, burned out, and weary from the grind as they try to survive toxic work cultures and climb the corporate ladder. Others can't commit to a career path and so jump from job to job, some in the name of chasing their passion and some for more "spiritual" reasons. Still others are chasing big dreams of being an "entrepreneur" and can't seem to find the secret sauce to make it all come together.

In so many of these conversations, I see and hear the same thing. People are looking for a way out of the struggle, a way around the challenges, a way that gets them ahead. They're looking for a shortcut to the job, career, and life of their dreams, and they're hoping I might have one to offer.

I completely get it. When I think back over the crises, hard work, long waits, and other difficulties I've faced over the years, both in my business and with my family, finances, health, and faith, there are many I have wished I could have somehow skipped, shortened, or made easier.

Yet there is the undeniable reality that these experiences have been what has formed me, my career, my relationship with God, and anything valuable I have to offer others.

And so, as people have shared their longings with me, my own longing for them has been growing to a crescendo, and I finally decided to write a book about it.

I don't want you to just have average relationships—I want you to thrive in them.

I don't want you to just find a job you love––I want you to find your purpose.

I don't want you to just suffer through hard work––I want you to fall in love with it.

I don't want you to find a way to just survive till the next promotion, job, or retirement––I want you to thrive in every season.

I don't want you to just know God—I want you to love Him with all your heart.

And I don't want to give you ~~SHORTCUTS~~ to your purpose, passion, and potential, because I know there are none. What I want to give you is courage and hope to embrace every step of your journey.

As the great John Maxwell said, "Shortcuts don't pay off in the long term. You'll never be all you can possibly be unless you embrace the process."

This is your life, and I don't want you to miss a moment of it.

Enjoy!

Bob
San Diego, California

"If you do the work you get rewarded. There are no shortcuts in life."

Michael Jordan

CHAPTER 1

Gaps

When I met 24-year-old Sabrina at a fundraising event, she quickly impressed me as being smart, energetic, and confident. As our conversation progressed, she opened up and began sharing her story with me. It started like a classic tale of the American dream. She had been raised by loving Christian parents who were also first-generation immigrants. Her father owned a small business and worked hard to give her everything she needed to succeed in life. Talented and driven, she was a top achiever through high school and inspired her teachers to comment that she would probably end up being the CEO of a company later in life. She studied science in college and graduated with honors. At twenty-two, she landed a summer internship with a leading biotech firm in Boston, and by the fall, she had been hired on to an entry-level position. She was on her way to a successful career in the biotech field.

By the dismissive way that Sabrina narrated these steps of her journey to me, however, I began to suspect that somewhere along the way, her dream job hadn't worked out the way she'd hoped. Sure enough, the next part of her story was marked by struggle, frustration, and disappointment. Sabrina explained that her biotech job had required her to put in sixty-plus-hour weeks doing tasks that she felt were repetitive, boring, and lacking in purpose. Her boss was critical, demanding, and totally uninterested in helping her grow and/or feel valued in her role. After making friends with a small group of work colleagues, she soon found their company to be a toxic mix of gossip, complaining, and cutthroat competition. Within a year, the honeymoon was completely over and Sabrina felt disillusioned and lost. The passion she had carried to work in biotech was gone, and she began to believe she was entirely on the wrong career path. Why continue to pour out her life in a job where there was no camaraderie or support, no sense of connection to a noble mission, and no clear path to promotion that didn't involve years of drudgery and climbing over other people's backs? She didn't just hate her job, she hated who she was becoming in it. It felt like all her compassion, hope, and idealism had been sucked out of her and she was on the verge of becoming like her colleagues—cynical, power hungry, and selfish.

"So what did you do?" I asked Sabrina.

"I quit," she replied. "I'm working part-time in the fashion industry right now. I'm still not sure what I want my career to look like, but I guess at least I know one thing I don't want to do."

I nodded and said I understood, but I couldn't help feeling troubled. Sabrina's was by no means the first story I had heard of a young person deciding to leave the job and career they'd trained for in college, but I couldn't help feeling there were aspects of her journey that could and perhaps should have been different. *Had she really picked the wrong career when she was obviously talented in science and technology?* I wondered. *Could she have found more effective ways of working with her boss and colleagues? Were her expectations about the job unrealistic? What if she had picked a different company with a different work culture? What if she had found better friends or a church community to support her in Boston?* Before I could ask Sabrina any of these questions, however, someone interrupted our conversation and whisked her away.

A few days after that fundraising event, I attended a Christian leadership conference. After one of the meetings, a smartly dressed young man, who appeared to be in his late thirties or early forties, approached me.

"Hey, Bob, I'm Lance," he said, grinning with confidence and extending his hand. "A mutual friend of ours over there told me I should meet you."

"Nice to meet you, Lance," I said, shaking his hand. "So why did this friend send you over here?"

"I just started a spiritual coaching business," Lance said. "I think he thought you might be interested in talking to me about it."

It sounded to me like Lance was about to ask me for some business advice, so I responded, "Okay, tell me a little more about your business."

"Well, I meet with business owners and CEOs, pray over them, and help them develop kingdom strategies for their businesses," he explained.

"Funny enough, I actually know a couple of people who do that," I smiled. "So how's it going and how can I help you?"

Lance's face lit up. "I would love to help *you*, Bob! How would you feel about me coming to your office to pray over you and your employees?"

I paused for a moment to decide how I should best reply to this direct and frankly off-putting pitch. I decided to ask Lance a few questions about his background. He explained that he had primarily worked in churches but decided to pivot into business after deciding he just wasn't into traditional pastoring anymore. He admitted that (unlike those I know who do Christian consulting) he had never run a business, owned a business, gone to business school, or mentored under someone in business. When I responded that it didn't sound like he had the kind of background to help me with my company, he tried to convince me that he didn't need a business background to do what he did for business owners. He then told me about several incidents where he had done "ministry" on site at several businesses. What he described was fairly alarming to me and I knew nothing like that would ever fly anywhere near my executive team or employees.

Finally, I said, as gently but honestly as I could, "Lance, I appreciate your enthusiasm, but I'm sorry to say everything you're telling me is a turnoff. I don't know you. You haven't asked me anything about my business. You haven't shown me evidence that you understand the kind of problems I need to solve or have experience or wisdom that I would find relevant or helpful. I think you're going to have a hard time winning business as a coach if this is your approach."

Lance looked shocked. After a moment he asked, "Are you being serious?"

"Absolutely," I nodded. "Thanks for the offer, but it's going to be a no from me."

"Oh . . ." Lance seemed even more surprised by my response than I had been by his offer. He smiled awkwardly, mumbled, "Well, thanks anyway," and hurried off.

Like my conversation with Sabrina, this encounter left me feeling troubled, for a couple reasons. First, there was Lance's apparent assumption that because we were both Christians and had a mutual friend, he could fast-track building trust and connection and get right to a transaction with me. There was his lack of awareness that until he built up more training and experience in his newly chosen field of business, someone with a mature business like mine probably won't be interested in hiring him. Finally, there was the fact that Lance didn't seem able to read me, pick up the significance of the questions I was asking him, and shift to a more curious and humble approach instead of doubling down on his pitch. I wasn't offended by these things—they made me feel badly for Lance. *Starting a new career and business in middle life is hard enough, but doing so without knowing how to build trust and credibility with people is going to be really rough,* I thought.

Within a week or so after returning from the leadership conference, a friend and business colleague from another state, Grant, reached out to me for some advice. He told me that the pastor of the small church he and his wife had faithfully attended for years was retiring. This man, Pastor Lewis, had often called on Grant, who owns a successful business, for advice on how to manage the church finances and to ask for financial help with both church initiatives and personal needs. This had created many uncomfortable situations for Grant. No matter how many times he sat down with Pastor Lewis to go through the church budget or opened his checkbook, it never seemed to translate into helping the pastor become a better financial manager or helping the church grow and become financially stable. Most of the initiatives he tried to start never got off the ground. Now, Grant had just learned that Pastor Lewis had no retirement to fall back on, having opted out of Social Security, saving, and investing over his entire career.

"I'm not sure what to do," Grant told me. "Pastor Lewis is good-hearted and well-loved by many people in our little church. At the same time, he just hasn't had any real vision, ambition, or work ethic. Again and again, he has coasted on the strength and support of those around him. He's been a mediocre leader and pastor, and it seems like I'm the only one who has ever challenged him to do better. He'll take my words to heart for a while but soon falls back into his old habits. Now he's in his late sixties with nothing to support him and his wife in their later years. I feel for him, but I also don't know how to help him."

I told Grant I empathized with his situation, and we discussed a few ideas for how to help Pastor Lewis and the church move toward a better future. After we hung up the phone, however, I once again felt troubled. *As a father, husband, and grandfather, I can't imagine what it must be like to retire with no means of providing for my family,* I thought. *I know God is my provider, but I also know it's His heart for us to build a legacy with what He gives us. It just doesn't seem right for a man to work for forty years and end up living on the charity of others.*

Noticing Gaps

Over the years I have encountered many people like Sabrina, Lance, and Pastor Lewis (I've changed their names to protect their privacy)—young people still living in their parents' homes who can't seem to "launch"; men and women in their twenties and thirties who tell me they have no passion for their jobs and dislike their bosses; self-described "visionaries" and "entrepreneurs" wanting to sell me on ideas that aren't thought-out and having no real strategy for how to make them happen; and friends and acquaintances in middle or later life who haven't built traction or achieved the kind of fruitfulness they should have been capable of producing in their careers. Nearly all of these people, as far as I knew, are believers with good hearts and intentions. But when they have shown me the way they approach their lives and work, I have noticed similar, troubling behavior patterns. Here are some of the most common:

- Complaints about a lack of "passion" for work or a specific job
- Quitting a job within two years of starting it
- Changing careers every couple years
- Living off the support of others for too long following seasons of training or education
- Expressing frustration about not advancing quickly enough in a career
- Mismanaging finances (living above one's means, impulse spending, etc.)
- Talking about dreams but never putting a successful plan into action

Behind these behaviors, there seemed to be a common set of beliefs, attitudes, and expectations. The expectation I most frequently heard from these people was that they should feel "passionate" about the work they did on a daily basis, coupled with the belief that a lack of passion meant they should find something else to do. Many of them would say that they felt "called" to something, but the moment they ceased to feel passionate about it, they would decide they must have missed their calling and needed to search for it elsewhere.

People in this group also frequently seemed to expect that they ought to be able to achieve their dream job at an accelerated pace. They typically—and quite rightly—hoped to rise to a level of mastery and leadership in a particular skill and role in a given field. But they seemed to think that the common path to that kind of success—starting in an entry level role, paying their dues by working hard at the lower-level tasks, and putting in years, even decades, of service—wasn't absolutely required in their case. In general, they didn't seem to have a value for cultivating traits like long-term vision, planning, perseverance, grit, or work ethic.

I also frequently noticed some kind of imbalance and compartmentalization between faith and work in their lives. Either faith appeared to be irrelevant to their work lives and they looked and sounded just like their non-Christian peers, or they seemed to fall into the old category of being "so spiritually minded that they're no earthly good" and couldn't translate their beliefs practically in the world of work. A common example of the latter was people who, as my friend Shawn Bolz puts it, used the "God card" to hustle people in the name of Jesus. This imbalance and compartmentalization manifested both in overwork, striving, and addiction to producing, and in laziness, passivity, and consumption. It also carried over into the way they approached other areas of their lives, such as relationships, finances, and their personal health.

Last, the people in this group had notable gaps in understanding themselves and others. Some couldn't recognize that their job was a bad fit for their personality and skill set. Others lacked the emotional and social skills to navigate the demands and expectations of people and communicate effectively in the workplace. And many could not see how much they were expecting their job or boss or colleagues to give them a sense of identity, purpose, connection, and significance they were missing.

Gaps Closed

As I ran back over my conversations with and observations of these people, I found myself drawing comparisons between them and a smaller but very different group of people—people who, instead of making me feel troubled, provoked feelings of excitement and admiration in me. I simply didn't see the same gaps in them.

The first person who came to mind was a man still in the first decade of his career, my friend Nick. I met Nick when he joined some friends and me at a business speakers' event, and he immediately impressed me with his humility, humor, intelligence, and easy confidence. I was shocked to learn that he was only in his early twenties. Nick knew at a young age that he wanted to work in finance, and specifically felt called to help people with financial stewardship. He also knew, largely due to watching his single mother struggle as an employee of a big corporation, that he wanted to start his own company. In high school, he sold nutritional products for a direct sales company and used the proceeds to open his first investment account. In college, he launched his first business, a technology education service, which ended up giving him capital to start the company he currently runs, a creative agency and alternative investment firm.

It always takes courage and grit to be an entrepreneur, but breaking into the financial services sector in your early twenties is especially challenging because a lot of people won't take you seriously. Along with plenty of rejection, which is normal in any business, Nick has weathered countless doubtful comments about his age and acumen in the process of winning the confidence and trust of his partners, colleagues, and clients. His ability to take all this in stride comes from being a man with great clarity of purpose, commitment to his mission, and hunger to grow and succeed.

The next person I thought of is a bit further along in her journey of life and work. My friend Katrina grew up on a fruit farm in rural Oregon and always felt called to carry on her family's farming legacy. Knowing that she would need to raise around a million dollars to buy the farm from her parents when they were ready to retire, she decided to go into healthcare, a field where she could serve people and make enough to raise that sum. Fifteen years later, she reached her savings goal and purchased the land. Immediately, she began expanding the farming operation from simple fruit production and sales to "farming, fermentation, and hospitality." To date, she has built a wedding venue, a tasting room/restaurant, and a facility to make beer, wine, and hard cider, tackling every challenge from getting permits to securing financing, managing the building projects, booking weddings and other events, staffing the restaurant, and marketing the businesses—all while still running the farm and working a day or two a week as a nurse practitioner. So far, all of these sub-businesses are thriving and have already transformed the once-struggling farm into a much healthier and very promising concern.

Last, I thought of someone in the third decade of his career—my banker, Victor. Victor and I met while serving on our kids' school board and later bonded when he helped Lauren and me manage the construction loan for our home. He's built a successful career at a national bank over the last twenty-five years, and credits the man who recruited him at his bank, and who is still his friend and mentor to this day, with challenging him to become the kind of banker who wouldn't just be an "order taker" for clients but who would actually advise them on what was best for their financial needs and objectives. To this day, he sees himself as a

"Joseph" who is privileged to serve "kings" as a wealth strategist. Good leadership, a healthy company culture, and the right role all created the opportunity for Victor's financial wisdom and servant leadership to develop and shine.

As I considered Nick, Katrina, Victor, and several other people in this second group (these are their real names, and I'll be introducing you to more of them throughout this book), I started to make a mental catalogue of the traits I saw in them.

First, they knew, with high levels of clarity and conviction, who they were and what they were called to do in life. In many cases, they had known this as early as middle or high school.

Next, they all carried a stewardship mindset. They believed their lives, calling, resources, and opportunities were gifts from God, and they were accountable to Him alone for how they used them.

They also had a partnership mindset. God was not a distant boss to them but was intimately involved in every step of their journey to fulfill what He had called them to do.

Undeniably, they all had the heart, mind, and posture of servants. They had dedicated their lives to serving their families, partners, employees, vendors, clients, and customers with their gifts, resources, knowledge, talents, and time.

They were also humble leaders possessing high levels of self-awareness, strong communication skills, healthy boundaries, and the ability to delegate or partner with others in areas where they weren't strong.

They also possessed every trait of the resilient. They were courageous and willing to risk failure. They repeatedly put themselves in situations that were over their heads and required them to be creative and resourceful. They were humble and hungry to learn, talked frankly about the mistakes they had made in their lives, loved and sought feedback, and were committed to personal growth. They consistently pushed through every form of resistance, from boredom to failure, to do their work.

Last, I noticed that this group of people happened to be some of the most joyful, passionate, powerful, and Christ-like people I know. They were both deeply spiritual and absolutely practical. They were both at rest in their identity and worked harder than most people on the planet. They carried both a long-term vision and the ability to be extremely focused in the present. In short, their faith grounded them and supported balance, health, and wholeness in every aspect of their lives.

The Core Difference

As I compared the two groups of people I've just described, I asked myself how I would summarize the central difference in their mindsets and behaviors. Here's what I landed on:

In general, both groups of people shared a similar desire and aspiration—to be successful in their career and to achieve a happy, meaningful, thriving life. However, the simplest way for me to put it is that the Sabrinas, Lances, and Pastor Lewises seemed to constantly be looking for *shortcuts* on the path to success and thriving. Dictionary.com defines "shortcut" as "a shorter or quicker way" and "a method, procedure, policy, etc., that reduces the time or energy needed to accomplish something." Their behavior displayed the belief that the path to success and thriving should be shorter, faster, and easier. Not just in their work or career, but in every area of life, from faith to relationships, health, and management of resources, they were always looking for the way of less or least resistance.

Meanwhile, the Nicks, Katrinas, and Victors, while they certainly looked for ways to learn, grow, improve, and become more efficient and effective in their work and life, didn't try to shortcut the process required to get them there. When they encountered resistance, they engaged it and pushed through it.

I have empathy for people in the first group, because in many ways they are simply following the script that is constantly being broadcast in today's culture. We live in a wealthy, technology and information-based society that is apparently obsessed with pursuing shortcuts. Our money and machines seem to promise that the time, energy, and resources required to achieve anything in life should be getting less and less, whether it's losing weight, getting our dream job, or making our first million. Hundreds of gurus of health, finance, business, and productivity promote shortcuts, "hacks," or "cheat codes" to gaining skills, the latest diet that gives "quick results," keys to achieving the "four-hour work week," or making profit in "three easy steps." The Western church has sometimes spiritualized this expectation, suggesting that because we are loved and favored by God and receive grace we could never earn, a life of following Him should be relatively smooth and easy. I know so many people who have struggled with bitterness and resentment toward God or even shipwrecked their faith when life gets hard, slow, and difficult, simply because they weren't expecting it.

But the second group understands that while money and machines can and do offer us certain shortcuts in life, they can't offer them for everything. In fact, they understand there are things you absolutely cannot shortcut in life, and that these are actually the most important things in life. Becoming the person you were created to be; achieving your dreams, realizing your potential, and fulfilling your calling; loving God, yourself, and others with all that you are—these *are* your life. And whenever you try to live it by grabbing at what is fast, short, and easy, you are not shortcutting your path; you are wandering from the path.

Wisdom Fills the Gaps

This fundamental ability to discern the difference between where it's appropriate to take shortcuts in life and where we cannot and must not take shortcuts is a function of *wisdom*. Wisdom is understanding God's design for our lives and living into that design, *taking the proven path by which that design unfolds*. It is the ability to apply His truth practically in all kinds of situations in a way that brings order, peace, and blessing. Wisdom is what produces good judgment, sound strategies, discernment, and healthy habits of spirit, mind, and body. Taking the proven path of wisdom is what leads not just to building a successful career, achieving our financial or health goals, or reaching our potential in faith, personal growth, and relationships, but to *thriving in life*.

How do we get wisdom? Wisdom comes to us in three primary ways. The one we are probably all most familiar with is *experience*. While experience in itself doesn't guarantee that we will learn from it, it is also true that only through experience does truth move from being mere ideas and information to becoming trained instincts, discernment, understanding, and skill. Second, wisdom comes to us from others who have gained wisdom through their experiences. Last, all wisdom ultimately comes from God through His Word and Spirit. Proverbs tells us that "the fear of the Lord"—that is, putting God in His rightful place as Lord and King, and trusting Him as the highest authority in our lives—is "the beginning of wisdom" (Proverbs 9:10). If we truly want to become wise, we will pursue wisdom from all of these sources.

However, we will only receive wisdom from these sources by taking the right posture—the posture of a learner, a student, a disciple. Solomon famously took this posture in his prayer for wisdom:

> Now, LORD my God, you have made your servant king in place of my father David. But I am only a little child and do not know how to carry out my duties. Your servant is here among the people you have chosen, a great people, too numerous to count or number. So give your servant a discerning heart to govern your people and to distinguish between right and wrong. For who is able to govern this great people of yours? (1 Kings 3:7-9, NIV)

Without exception, the wisest people I know all demonstrate this humble, hungry heart of a learner, no matter their age or experience. They never conclude that they have "arrived" and can stop seeking wisdom. *And yet*, the wisest people are also those who seem so far ahead of most people when it comes to thriving in life. Why? Wisdom is *not* a shortcut—it doesn't bypass the process of learning, growth, and hard work. But, because it helps you embrace and navigate that process successfully, wisdom actually *does* accelerate you, make you more effective, and save you time in learning to thrive in life. This is why people like Nick, Victor, and Katrina stand out from the crowd—not because they are the kind of people the world defines as "success stories," but because they are truly thriving.

In a recent conversation with Nick, we were discussing the way he interacts with many of the mentors and advisors in his life. He told me that in high school he had heard a quote: "A smart man learns from his own mistakes. A wise man learns from others." He took this to heart and made a commitment to seek out people ahead of him who had walked through each stage of building a financial business. While most young entrepreneurs feel pressure to go it alone and make a name for themselves, Nick has pursued successful people in his field and humbly asked them to walk him through their experience. "You have to take out pride," he admitted to me. "But when you do, the learning curve gets drastically sped up. I'm now able to meet with clients and offer far more tested knowledge and insight than I would have been able trying to figure things out on my own."

That sounds a little like a shortcut, doesn't it? It's just not a shortcut many people take or find attractive, because for most of us, humbling ourselves and sitting under the influence of those who are older and wiser are psychologically and spiritually challenging. It's not easy. And yet those willing to do this hard thing find that it pays off by making things easier down the road.

This is the paradox of shortcuts. If we chase shortcuts that promise to make life easy, we wander from the proven path to thriving. But if we do the difficult work of filling the gaps in our wisdom, we stay on the proven path and build momentum to thriving. Here's one way to put it: *The only true shortcuts in life come through filling our gaps in wisdom.*

One of the reasons people like Nick impress me so much is that they identify the gaps in their wisdom much earlier than many of us do, and they go after filling them. We all have wisdom gaps that need to be filled—that's the whole point of our journey to mature as sons and daughters of God. Unfortunately, many believers are totally unaware that what they are fundamentally lacking is not passion or the right job or a better work environment but *wisdom for life*. As long as they are misidentifying the true gap in their lives, they will continue to try to solve the wrong problem. This is why so many of them are not thriving as they can and should.

To be clear, the reason I hold up examples like Sabrina, Lance, and Pastor Lewis to you is not to judge or condemn them. Again, we all have wisdom gaps to fill, and I am no different. I certainly have made tons of unwise decisions throughout my life. However, the real danger for all of us is that, instead of coming back to a posture of humility and learning, we take the opposite posture of resisting wisdom when it is offered to us and insisting that we don't need to change, grow, and improve. Believe me, I get it—humility, adjustment, and growth are uncomfortable and hard. But avoiding them shapes us into something so much worse. While I have to hold on to hope that every person, at any point in their life, can choose to repent from this posture of pride and rejection of wisdom, make an about-face, and change, I have also seen what happens to people who reach the later years of their life without ever doing so. They end up as broken, dysfunctional, bitter, empty narcissists who never took the path to a thriving life, and instead end up leaving a legacy of pain in the lives of those who know them. This is not who we want to be.

Here is something I know with absolute confidence. In the kingdom of God, people like Nick, Katrina, and Victor are not meant to be the exception but the rule. The Father wants each and every one of His children to know who they are and what they are called to do. He wants us to work and live with passion and perseverance. He wants us to succeed and thrive and be fruitful. And He wants to partner with us every step of the way. But the only way to do this is, as the writer of Proverbs instructs us, to "get wisdom" (Proverbs 4:5).

In the pages ahead, my goal is to give you the best of what I have learned through my own experiences, from others, and from the Spirit and Word of God about how we become people of wisdom who live into God's design and take the proven path to the abundant, thriving life He desires for us. Here's the basic map for our journey together:

- First, we'll take a look at our cultural moment and identify some of the big problems in the world's prevailing wisdom on the path of success in work and life. (chapter 2)
- Next, we'll dive into Scripture and learn some essential truths about God's grand design and purpose for our work and life. (chapter 3)
- We'll connect that grand design with our own lives and see how important it is to gain clarity on our identity, purpose, and assignments. (chapter 4)
- Then we'll look at how passion is actually connected to what we do, and how to experience it in our work and life. (chapter 5)
- We'll explore four essential aspects of our journey to finding the roles where we can grow, thrive, and contribute our best work to the world: personality and gifts, execution, culture, and character. (chapter 6)
- Then we'll focus on how our purpose and passion in life are inextricably connected with people, and how stewarding our relationships well is critical to the path of wisdom. (chapter 7)
- We'll look at how the proven path of wisdom tells us to approach work-life balance. (chapter 8)
- We'll dive into the essential truths we must embrace to become wise managers of our time, energy, and money. (chapter 9)

- Finally, we'll explore key principles in the art of planning and personal growth that enable us to build a legacy of wisdom. (chapter 10)

As we take this journey together, I pray you will find important pieces of wisdom that will help you identify and begin to close your gaps so you can start thriving in your work and in life.

"Pray like it all depends on God, but work like it all depends on you."

Dave Ramsey

CHAPTER 2

The World Is Out of Balance

L iving in God's wisdom for our lives involves learning the art of *balance*. Life is full of tension, and wisdom shows us how to balance these areas of tension in a way that leads to thriving. Conversely, when we are not thriving—when our lives start to break down with anxiety, depression, relational dysfunction, burnout, fatigue, illness, addiction, etc.—then we can be sure that it is because we are not balancing these areas of tension well.

One of the most critical tensions we wrestle with as Christians is living both as citizens of the kingdom of God and citizens of a world that has yet to become fully restored to God's original design: on Earth as it is in heaven. When believers live in this tension wisely, it produces Christ-like transformation, first in us personally, and then through us in the world. When we don't, classically two things happen: we either become like the world, or we attempt to distance ourselves from the world in some kind of separate religious culture.

The fact that we see so many Christians—ourselves included—pulled in these two directions speaks to how difficult it is to balance this tension. It's easier to go with the flow of the world or try to create our own safe place where everyone believes what we believe. It's much harder to live and work in a culture with opposite values, beliefs, and behaviors. It's harder to bravely allow Jesus to send us out as "sheep in the midst of wolves" and learn how to "be wise as serpents and harmless as doves" than it is to simply stay away from the wolves or be consumed by them (Matthew 10:16, NKJV). It's hard to balance the tension of loving the world like Jesus (see John 3:16) and yet not loving the world (see 1 John 2:15). But taking this hard path is the only way to the thriving, free, abundant life Jesus has for us.

When I consider the wisdom gaps I see in many Christians, specifically in their attitudes and approach to their work, jobs, and career, I believe these gaps are rooted in their inability to balance this tension well. As I said, I meet many believers who are either too indistinguishable from nonbelievers or are too out of touch with the world due to living in some Christian "bubble." Conversely, much of the wisdom I see in people like Nick, Katrina, and Victor is expressed in their ability to live and work in both realities with consistency, grace, and integrity. I would argue that ability is grounded primarily in two things: a good, biblical theology of work, and good discernment about where American work culture aligns with truth and where it distorts the truth.

In the next chapter, we'll dive into the Bible's wisdom on work. But first I want to take a look at today's work culture and start to identify some of the big signs that it is obviously off-balance. The very fact that work-life balance has become such a big topic in the last decade or so suggests that our lack of balance has become glaringly obvious to many people. As believers, I think we need to see this as an opportunity. The world is looking for a vision of what a balanced life looks like, and we have unique access to the only source of wisdom that can lead them to that vision. However, we will not lead anyone anywhere as long as we are trying to follow the current cultural narrative for how to work and live. People are not going to fix their work-life balance problem solely by setting better goals, designing their day to be more productive, developing a self-care routine, taking more vacations, or getting more maternity or paternity leave. We have to go both deeper and wider than these behavioral strategies. We need to go after understanding the core beliefs, desires, and motives of the heart and God's grand design and purpose for our lives. Only then can we bring our behavior and habits into proper alignment. So let's start by looking at how the wider culture is approaching work today and noting some of the ways it's missing the mark.

The Evolution of the American Work Ethic

Growing up, I learned that our nation was founded on the ideals of virtuous capitalism and the Protestant work ethic. As a society, we have always believed that it is better for individuals to have ownership and responsibility for their life, land, and property. Possessing means of production and a stewardship mindset naturally motivates people to work hard to grow and manage what they have, which in turn can produce wealth and lead to human flourishing. This is the ideal behind the American dream—the dream that every person, regardless of their status, should have a chance to make something better of their lives.

In two-and-a-half centuries of pursuing these ideals, we've seen both success and failure, tremendous good as well as great injustice. There is no doubt that we have become one of the most productive and prosperous nations in the world. Our recent decades of economic growth have been largely fueled by the rise of computing, automation, digital communication technology, and the internet, which has transitioned us from an industrial to an information economy. But all our productivity and prosperity have created their own challenges. One of our greatest challenges has been trying to understand and respond well to changing expectations and motivations around work.

Pastor and author John Mark Comer offers this summary description of how our expectations of work have changed over the past few generations:

I'm a millennial . . .

> Our grandparents' generation grew up during the Great Depression, and then lived through World War 2. They were just happy to have a job. Safety and security was a high enough goal to shoot for. If they could pay the mortgage and put food on the table, they were happy.

> Our parents' generation took it one step further. They wanted more than a steady job that could pay the bills. They wanted to make money. A lot of it. Buy stuff. Play. Go on vacation somewhere tropical.

> But my generation left the atmosphere. We aren't happy with just a high-paying job, a nice car, and the occasional

expensive vacation. We want our dreams to come true. We want fulfillment from our work.[1]

I admit that I fall more or less in the middle of those three categories. Unlike Nick and Katrina, I didn't grow up with any clear idea of what I wanted or felt called to do with my life. I went off to college believing I'd find a career path that suited me, started painting houses as a side job, realized I could make a living with painting, and decided to stop going to school and focus full-time on building a painting business. I recognized that I had found an opportunity to perform a service that was in demand, which I had the skill to do with excellence and efficiency, and liked doing well enough. I *did* enjoy the process and reward of transforming the spaces in which people lived and worked, and when the demand grew beyond my capacity and I started to build a team, it was also gratifying to discover that I also loved and had a gift for leadership and collaboration. But the most rewarding thing to me was that I could build a profitable business and create a means for me and my employees to make a good living for our families.

Over forty years, my company grew from one guy—me—painting houses out of a Volkswagen Bug to a mature contractor serving the industrial/commercial construction sector of the southwestern United States. I never had any kind of get-rich-quick scheme or shortcut to becoming an overnight success. It took thirty years before we hit our first grand slam as a company and were able to scale up significantly, and I give God credit for that because it happened at the start of the 2008 recession, and there's no way I could have planned it the way it happened—I

---

1 John Mark Comer, *Garden City: Work, Rest, and the Art of Being Human* (Grand Rapids, MI: Zondervan, 2015), 170-171.

am just not that smart. But there's also no doubt that building, growing, and running a mature business only happened through sustained hard work. I never imagined that it could be otherwise.

Not surprisingly, the type of imbalance I fell into at various points in those forty years was classic overwork and workaholism. Many times, I crossed that line where I was carrying the weight of the business fully on my shoulders, and I wasn't operating from trust in God. I became stressed, anxious, and isolated. I didn't know how to stop, rest, and recover. I was neglecting my spiritual, physical, and emotional health, as well as my family. And so I had to recognize where I was operating out of the worldly wisdom of self-sufficiency and pulling myself up by my bootstraps rather than the wisdom of God, and move back toward living in balance.

Today when I talk with people who are in the first third or so of their work life or career, I see the shift in their expectations around work. While I still meet plenty of people like me who like working hard and can slip out of balance into overwork, I also meet lots of people who are struggling to value hard work for various reasons. Some of these are children of workaholics who sacrificed their families on the altar of their own success. But I think a large number of them are struggling because of this cultural shift toward adding "dreams coming true" and "fulfillment" to our definition of success.

Balance Issues: Wealth, Scarcity, Competition, Anxiety, and Burnout

In one respect, I think this shift reflects the reality of becoming wealthier as a nation. And I think there are few who would argue that this kind of progress is a bad thing. The journey from survival to material wealth to personal fulfillment tracks with our increased ability as a society to ascend Maslow's hierarchy of needs.[2]

The fact that the current priority for many people beginning their careers is to find their "dream job" doing something they find personally fulfilling suggests that their more basic physical and psychological needs are being met. And speaking as a dad, I absolutely support that priority. I want my kids to dream and pursue their dreams. I want the things they spend most of their waking hours doing to be deeply fulfilling and rewarding to them. I absolutely don't want them to drag through life in survival mode, bored to death by mind-numbing tasks, lacking any sense of purpose or passion for their work.

But as we encourage people to find their "dream job," the very wealth of material resources and opportunities that makes this possible can also hurt their ability to dream, simply by making them too comfortable to risk the discomfort required to pursue and realize those dreams. Malcolm Gladwell described this downside in his book *David and Goliath*. He interviewed a wildly successful Hollywood mogul who worked his way up from blue-collar roots to Beverly Hills. At some point in their conversation, this man described to Gladwell the problem he was now facing as a parent:

> He has children that he loved very dearly. Like any parent, he wanted to provide for them, to give them more than he had. But he had created a giant contradiction, and he knew it. He was successful because he had learned the long and hard way about the value of

2 "Maslow's Hierarchy of Needs," Saul McCleod, www.SimplePsychology.org, last updated March 20, 2020, https://www.simplypsychology.org/maslow.html

money and the meaning of work and the joy and fulfillment that come from making your own way in the world. But because of his success, it would be difficult for his children to learn those same lessons . . .

"My own instinct is that it's much harder than anybody believes to bring up kids in a wealthy environment," he said. "People are ruined by challenged economic lives. But they're ruined by wealth as well because they lose their ambition and they lose their pride and they lose their sense of self-worth. It's difficult at both ends of the spectrum. There's some place in the middle which probably works best of all."[3]

Gladwell goes on to explain that this parenting problem is not historically new:

The psychologist James Grubman uses the wonderful expression "immigrants to wealth" to describe first-generation millionaires—by which he means that they face the same kinds of challenges in relating to their children that immigrants to any new country face. Someone like the Hollywood mogul grew up in the Old Country of the middle class, where scarcity was a great motivator and teacher. His father taught him the meaning of money and the virtues of independence and hard work. But

3 Malcolm Gladwell, *David and Goliath* (New York, NY: Little, Brown and Company, 2013), 47.

his children live in the New World of riches, where the rules are different and baffling. How do you teach "work hard, be independent, learn the meaning of money" to children who look around themselves and realize that they never have to work hard, be independent, or learn the meaning of money? That's why so many cultures around the world have a proverb to describe the difficulty of raising children in an atmosphere of wealth. In English, the saying is "Shirtsleeves to shirtsleeves in three generations." The Italians says, "*Dalle stelle alle stalle*" ("from stars to stables"). In Spain it's "*Quien no lo tiene, lo hance; y quien lo teine, lo deshance*" ("he who doesn't have it, does it, and he who has it, misuses it"). Wealth contains the seeds of its own destruction.[4]

I realize that few of us belong in the same category as the Hollywood mogul and his kids, but I do believe that many people today are struggling to find and commit to a career because they have so many options and are living comfortably enough that there is less urgency for them to pick one. The world of wealth and opportunity in which they live, which was built through hard work, gives them an automatic leg up, or shortcut, to their dreams, yet at the same time it can discourage them from committing to their own journey of hard work. If they really want to find a deeply fulfilling job, they will probably need to experience a kind of scarcity or need that will help them build the character of sacrifice, grit, hard work, and thriftiness, which sets them up to experience genuine reward and satisfaction. I'm not suggesting that to find a meaningful

4 Ibid., 50-51.

career we need to choose poverty or try to pull ourselves up totally by our own bootstraps. I am saying that great careers only come to those who are willing to embrace certain *limits*—the kind of limits that actually cause us to focus on identifying and running after what we are uniquely designed and called to do by God on this earth.

However, our culture is moving in the opposite direction. Many parents these days continue to tell their kids, "You can be whatever you want to be and do whatever you want when you grow up." But this isn't exactly true. While it is wonderful to encourage children to dream and discover the desires of their heart, it is wrong to leave out that there are very real limits to what it will mean for them to pursue those desires. There are limits created by their own personalities, skills, and abilities, and the process by which those things can develop into maturity and mastery. There are limits created by their family and community. There are limits inherent in the nature of whatever career or job they want to pursue. And there are limits in the job market and economy. Many people seem to be growing up without having someone help them discover both their potential and the practical limits to reaching it, which sets them up for frustration when they bump into those limits.

Many parents, along with popular culture, have encouraged kids to be the "best" at something, while celebrating as examples those who have achieved mastery and super-success in their field, often in what seems to be a short amount of time (tech geniuses, pop stars, athletes, etc.). I am all about excellence and believe that we all have the potential and mandate to reach for *our individual best*, which is inherently glorious because we are made in the image of God. However, setting the bar for everyone at superstar level is a recipe for hyper-competition and all that comes with it—comparison, jealousy, posturing, and conformity.

Social media has come to play a big role in people's quest to become—or at least to appear as—superstars. Facebook, Instagram, and Twitter have become the marketplace where people broadcast their own highlight reel of material success, personal fulfillment, and being the "best." The moment that advertising companies saw how these curated images of success were *already* marketing to consumers, they jumped into bed with the tech companies to capture the real money to be made by people driven by the deep need and desire to be—or at least seem to be—successful. I believe this is one of the primary causes of debt and overspending in this generation. We live beyond our means largely because we want what others have and we want to appear successful.

However, behind the social media "success pageant" is the reality that our culture of hyper-achievement and competition is triggering deep insecurities in many of us. Brené Brown argues that one of the primary outgrowths of this insecurity is the epidemic of narcissism that seems to afflict so many today:

> When I look at narcissism through the vulnerability lens, I see **the shame-based fear of being ordinary.** I see the fear of never being extraordinary enough to be noticed, to be lovable, to belong, or to cultivate a sense of purpose . . . I see the cultural messaging everywhere that says an ordinary life is a meaningless life. And I see how kids that grow up on a steady diet of reality television, celebrity culture, and unsupervised social media can absorb this messaging and develop a completely skewed

sense of the world. *I am only as good as the number of "likes" I get on Facebook or Instagram.*[5]

This pressure to be extraordinary in a world where we are constantly comparing ourselves to the best of the best contributes to what Brown describes as our "culture of scarcity," the constant, nagging belief that we are never enough. I think there's a lesson here. Scarcity is something we will experience, no matter how much material wealth we attain. We can either embrace the healthy scarcity of our God-given limits, which happens to be the only way to really live into the truth that we are enough and there is enough, or we can try to run after the world's perpetual, insecurity-inducing scarcity that comes when we are trying to be, do, and have it all.

In addition to driving so many of us to build and manage our images on social media, our culture of scarcity is responsible, I believe, for contributing to the rising levels of anxiety we see in our society as a whole. Journalist Malcolm Harris describes how this anxiety is affecting the way we approach work:

> Given what we know about the recent changes in the American sociocultural environment, it would be a surprise if there weren't elevated levels of anxiety among young people. Their lives center around production, competition, surveillance, and achievement in ways that were totally exceptional only a few decades ago. All this striving, all this trying to catch up and stay ahead—it

---

5 Brené Brown, *Daring Greatly* (New York, NY: Penguin, 2012), 27.

simply has to have psychological consequences. The symptoms of anxiety aren't just the unforeseen and unfortunate outcome of increased productivity and decreased labor costs; they're *useful*... Our hypercompetitive society pushes children's performance up, and their common level of anxiety with it. The kind of production required from kids requires attention, and lots of it. The environment aggressively selects at every level for kids who can maintain an optimum level of arousal and performance without going over the metaphorical (or literal) edge...

Our society runs headlong into an obvious contradiction when it tries to turn "high-achieving" into "normal." The impossibility of the demand that people, on average, be better than average, doesn't excuse any individual child's average—or, God forbid!, subpar—performance. The gap between expectations and reality when it comes to the distribution of American life outcomes is anxiety-inducing, and it's supposed to be. Anxiety is productive, up to a limit.[6]

I think we see two basic reactions to this cultural anxiety. The first reaction is the "hustle" culture, the new face of overwork and workaholism, which for many workers today is driven not only by the desire to find a dream job and achieve greatness but also by the pressure to pay

6 Malcolm Harris, *Kids These Days* (New York, NY: Little, Brown and Company), 167-169.

off student loan debt and maintain a comfortable lifestyle. In her viral essay "How Millennials became the burnout generation," Anne Helen Peterson described how she found herself in this type of overwork:

> As I continued through grad school, I accumulated more and more debt—debt that I rationalized, like so many of my generation, as the only means to achieve the end goal of 1) a "good" job that would 2) be or sound cool and 3) allow me to follow my "passion." In this case, full-time, tenure-track employment as a media studies professor.

> In the past, pursuing a PhD was a generally debt-free endeavor: Academics worked their way toward their degree while working as teaching assistants, which paid them cost of living and remitted the cost of tuition. That model began to shift in the 1980s, particularly at public universities forced to compensate for state budget cuts. Teaching assistant labor was far cheaper than paying for a tenured professor, so the universities didn't just keep PhD programs, but expanded them, even with dwindling funds to adequately pay those students. Still, thousands of PhD students clung to the idea of a tenure-track professorship. And the tighter the academic market became, the harder we worked. We didn't try to break the system, since that's not how we'd been raised. We tried to *win* it.

> I never thought the system was equitable. I knew it was

winnable for only a small few. I just believed I could continue to optimize myself to become one of them . . . Grad school, then, is where I learned to work like a millennial, which is to say, all the time. My new watchword was "Everything that's good is bad, everything that's bad is good": Things that should've felt good (leisure, not working) felt bad because I felt guilty for not working; things that should've felt "bad" (working all the time) felt good because I was doing what I thought I should and needed to be doing in order to succeed.

Peterson goes on to describe how the pressure to create a social media narrative of success and distinction, or a "personal brand," as well as tech-based accessibility to every hour of her life, even those that were supposed to be "rest" or "play," supported this "total work" lifestyle:

"Branding" is a fitting word for this work, as it underlines what the millennial self becomes: a product. And as in childhood, the work of optimizing that brand blurs whatever boundaries remained between work and play. There is no "off the clock" when at all hours you could be documenting your on-brand experiences or tweeting your on-brand observations. The rise of smartphones makes these behaviors frictionless and thus more pervasive, more standardized. In the early days of Facebook, you had to take pictures with your digital camera, upload them to your computer, and post them in albums. Now, your phone is a sophisticated camera, always ready to document every component of your life—in easily manipulated photos, in short video bursts, in constant updates to Instagram Stories—and to facilitate the labor of performing the self for public consumption.

But the phone is also, and just as essentially, a tether to the "real" workplace. Email and Slack make it so that employees are always accessible, always able to labor, even after they've left the physical workplace and the traditional 9-to-5 boundaries of paid labor. Attempts to discourage working "off the clock" misfire, as millennials read them not as permission to stop working, but a means to further distinguish themselves by being available anyway.[7]

For people who embrace this path of overwork, Peterson says, the result is living in a state of constant, lingering, low-grade burnout. What is more, she argues that the attempts to treat this burnout with therapy, medication, and self-care—niches that have exploded in recent years, largely in response to widespread burnout—do not address the deeper causes for it. The growing conversations around work-life balance, the need for corporations to have some kind of social-justice mission, and even the renewal of interest in democratic socialism are all reactions to the pressures and burnout many people feel in today's work

7 Anne Helen Peterson, "How Millennials Became the Burnout Generation," *Buzzfeed*, January 5, 2019, https:/www.buzzfeednews.com/article/annehelenpetersen/ millennials-burnout-generation-debt-work.

culture—but none of them are solutions that get to the root of what is driving our anxiety.

However, not everyone reacts to our cultural anxiety by digging in and trying to "win" the system through overwork. Many people find the high expectations, intense competition, and risk of failure and disappointment simply too overwhelming or paralyzing to face. These people are choosing the path of underwork, which has given rise to stereotypes of people living off their parents' support much longer than they need to find a job, or moving from job to job in a never-ending quest to find their dream job.

The Church and Work Culture

When I look at the church, at least the streams of it with which I'm most familiar, I see plenty of signs that we have been buying into the world's wisdom around work. My generation produced the workaholic pastors who built megachurches, and the next generation of church leadership has been marked by the celebrities and superstars with their branded ministry platforms. However, as many of these leaders have failed morally, crashed due to stress or anxiety, or even committed suicide, the conversation around "ministry burnout" has picked up steam.

When it comes to church attenders, many of them have heard a message similar to "You can be anything you want to be and be great at it," which sounds like "You're called to dream big, do great things, and change the world for God." While this message isn't wrong in principle (and we'll explore it further in this book), it seems that many believers have interpreted it through the wider culture's definitions of what it means to do something "great" and "change the world." This leads many of them to see becoming a spiritual rock star, achieving financial success, and building a social media platform as the primary means of influencing culture and advancing the kingdom of God.

In short, much of the church is struggling in the same way the world is—not necessarily because we are wanting wrong things, but because we are not living out God's wisdom for how to get the good things He wants us to have. The desires for security, significance, achievement, financial success, excellence, and fulfillment are all core to who He designed and called us to be. This is why, when Jesus' disciples fell into an argument over which of them was the greatest, He didn't rebuke them but showed them God's definition of and path to greatness:

> The kings and men of authority in this world rule oppressively over their subjects, claiming that they do it for the good of the people. They are obsessed with how others see them. But this is not your calling. You will lead by a different model. The greatest one among you will live as one called to serve others without honor. The greatest honor and authority is reserved for the one who has a servant heart. The leaders who are served are the most important in your eyes, but in the kingdom, it is the servants who lead. Am I not here with you as one who serves you? (Luke 22:25-27, TPT)

As followers of Jesus, we are called to recognize that the world's strategy for pursuing our core needs and desires will always diverge from God's strategy for our lives, and that at the deepest level, this is the source of all our frustration, disappointment, and disillusionment. The only path to true passion, success, and fulfillment lies in discovering how to work, rest, and live according to our Father's design.

"My Father is always at his work to this very day, and I too am working."

Jesus (John 5:17)

CHAPTER 3

God's Wisdom for Work and Life

A s I said at the beginning of the last chapter, the challenge we face as
believers is to avoid either conforming to or separating ourselves
from the world, and instead to position ourselves so that our lives give
people an opportunity to experience the culture of the kingdom. We
are the ones called to show them that there's a better option than either
getting sucked into the wider culture of greed, consumption, competition, jealousy, hustling, anxiety, and burnout, or trying to escape from
it all in Alaska or a monastery. However, we can't offer this better option
unless we are living in it ourselves, and we can't live in it without fully
embracing a biblical worldview.

If I were to try to distill the biblical worldview on work down to its
simplest formulation, I would argue that it is all built on these two fundamental principles:

- Everything is spiritual/sacred.
- We were created to be God's apprentices.

Understanding these two principles helps us to confront the two main false beliefs that have held far too many believers back in their ability to demonstrate the kingdom of God in their lives, especially in their work.

The Sacred/Secular Split

The Bible tells us that God created the universe and called it good. Even when humans rebelled and followed the enemy, God didn't abandon or destroy the earth and start over but has been patiently at work throughout human history to bring us back to Him and restore all things. The Bible repeatedly affirms that everything in the universe belongs to Him and that He upholds and reigns over it all. He is not some distant, uninterested God but is passionately participating in every aspect of this universe, even though so often we are blind to Him. This is why the classical Jewish and Christian view of the universe is that everything—including every aspect of human life and experience—is spiritual, in the sense that it was made by God for His purposes, belongs to Him, and can't escape the laws and limits of His reality.

However, humans have always had a habit of "suppressing the truth" (Romans 1:18) and trying to come up with their own version of reality and explanation for why the world is the way it is. One of the oldest of these human philosophies is dualism, which first became popular in Greco-Roman culture hundreds of years before Christ came to Earth. The Greeks believed that reality had two basic dimensions: the ideal or spiritual, which was pure and good, and the material or physical, which was dirty and corrupt. This gave rise to the idea that the "good life" was one spent as detached as possible from the mundane activities of the physical world. They saw work as a curse and divided their society into classes with common laborers, who did the jobs that were considered the least spiritual or noble, at the bottom, and elite philosophers, who sat around all day discussing ideas and truth, at the top.

Once the Christian church became more Gentile than Jewish, this dualistic worldview took hold and created a belief in what many call the *sacred/secular split*. Many Christians began to believe that certain activities were spiritual (or sacred) and other activities were not spiritual, and that the spiritual activities must be more important and have greater eternal value than non-spiritual activities. This gave rise to divisions and hierarchies in the church between sacred and secular, spiritual and physical, clergy and laity, and more. Martin Luther famously confronted this problem during the Reformation, proclaiming that in God's eyes, these divisions and hierarchies should not exist. He called the church back to the biblical view of the world, teaching that every believer is a priest to God and man, that every believer has a calling, and that all work done unto the Lord is sacred.

However, while the Reformation succeeded in breaking up the extreme excesses of the sacred/secular split culture in the Catholic Church and inspired many Christians with a sense of divine calling and stewardship in their everyday jobs—which produced the Protestant work ethic—it did not end the sacred/secular split within the church or dualism in the wider culture. It is likely that as long as we find ourselves in the tension of living in a world that has not yet fully come under the rule and reign of God, the temptation to fall into this worldview will be there.

One expression of the sacred/secular split I have seen affect many people in my generation originates in the "left behind" teaching on the end times. This teaching has led many to think that the only work that really matters for Christians is getting people "saved" so they will be ready for the Rapture. Those who have taken this to an extreme have given up making any long-term plans for their lives because they expect Jesus to come back at any moment and destroy the earth. Why go to college, work hard at some "secular" job, and save money for retirement when "it's all going to burn"? Sadly, all this teaching has led many believers to withdraw their service and influence from the world and contribute to Christianity becoming marginalized in our society.

Other expressions of the sacred/secular split I have seen fall along more classical lines. Even though in our modern Protestant, Evangelical, and Charismatic/Pentecostal churches we no longer ascribe to philosophical hierarchies, in practice many of our cultures encourage the idea that those whose full-time profession it is to teach and preach the Bible, lead praise and worship on Sunday mornings, go on missions to foreign countries, teach in a Bible college or seminary, or do any other number of jobs traditionally called "religious," "spiritual," or "ministry," are doing spiritual jobs, while the rest of us are doing secular jobs. These definitions cause problems when church leaders try to fulfill Paul's instruction in Ephesians 4 to "equip the saints for the work of ministry" (v. 12, ESV). It typically leads them to define "ministry" or "works of service" narrowly as things like teaching, preaching, praying, prophesying, tithing, going to church, singing worship songs, or evangelism. Believers learn either that they are only supposed to do these things at church events or that "ministering in the workplace" means doing things on that list of ministry activities at their jobs.

I don't know if you found my response to Lance's request to come "minister" at my business in chapter 1 a little too direct or even harsh, but it comes out of my long history of experience encountering believers who operate with this understanding of "work" and "ministry." And I can tell you that it generally does not succeed in presenting a compelling invitation for people to encounter the kingdom of God in the workplace. If Lance had been hungrier to learn where his approach was off, I might have had the opportunity to share some stories of people I know who have tried to minister in their workplace, did not have good results, and learned a better way.

For example, I was at a conference with my friend Shawn Bolz when a man named Jeff came up to talk to me. He told me a story about an earlier time in his life when he was young, zealous, but lacking in wisdom about "ministry in the workplace." A friend from church who was a contractor gave Jeff a job on one of his construction crews. Since his boss was a Christian, Jeff assumed he had *carte blanche* to spend as much work time as he "felt led" telling the guys on the work crew about Jesus and asking to pray for them. When neither the boss nor his work colleagues responded well to him talking so much about God, he decided to take his boss to coffee and confront him over the way he was running his business, telling him that his focus shouldn't just be on getting the job done but also "ministering" to each other. He was shocked when his boss responded by letting him go. Thankfully, Jeff told me, he learned from this experience and discovered that working hard with excellence was just as much "ministry" as praying for people, and that this was what God expected of him at a job.

Another, more subtle, expression of the sacred/secular split I see in the church comes from those who believe that the church should influence and shape the wider culture but who think that can only happen if they hold certain positions of leadership or do certain kinds of work. In this, they often align with the dualistic elitism that still shapes many of the attitudes toward work in American culture. Tim Keller describes some of these attitudes:

> One is that work is a necessary evil. The only good work, in this view, is work that helps make us money so that we can support our families and pay others to do menial work. Second, we believe that lower-status or lower-paying work is an assault on our dignity. One result of this belief is that many people take jobs that they are not suited for at all, choosing to aim for careers that do not fit their gifts but promise higher wages and prestige. Western societies are increasingly divided between the highly remunerated "knowledge classes" and the more poorly remunerated "service sector," and most of us accept and perpetuate the value judgments that attach to these categories. Another result is that many people will choose to be unemployed rather than do work that they feel is beneath them, and most service and manual labor falls into this category. Often people who have made it into the knowledge classes show great disdain for the concierges, handymen, dry cleaners, cooks, gardeners, and others who hold service jobs.[8]

8 Timothy Keller, *Every Good Endeavor: Connecting Your Work to God's Work* (New York, NY: Penguin Books, 2016), 34-35.

By far, I think these subtler attitudes are the most destructive versions of the sacred/secular split or dualistic thinking, and we can *all* slip into them if we're not careful. Unless we are anchored in the wisdom of God for our work, we will inevitably compartmentalize our faith and work, negatively compare our work to others, fail to see the redemptive purpose and reward of our work, miss our true calling, and never experience the fulfilling and fruitful life of work God desires for us.

"Work Is a Curse"

The second false belief about work that continues to beset many Christians is that we have to work because of the fall. It seems to be a favorite excuse to bring out when someone wants to complain about their work being hard, boring, long, frustrating, underpaid, or unsatisfying in some way. "Well, work is part of the curse." People who believe this imagine that if humans had never sinned, we'd all still be lounging around naked in the Garden of Eden eating and drinking and enjoying lives of total leisure. This is also what they imagine heaven will be like. Unfortunately, this is that old Greek view of work, leisure, and the afterlife, not the Bible's view. The Bible clearly shows that work was *not* part of the fall or curse but was part of God's original design for humans.

Genesis introduces God as a master craftsman who *works*: "And on the seventh day God ended His work which He had done" (Genesis 2:2, NKJV). In His final act of creation, the master craftsman creates His own family of apprentices to join Him in His work:

> Then God said, "Let Us make man in Our image, according to Our likeness; let them have dominion over the fish of the sea, over the birds of the air, and over the

cattle, over all the earth and over every creeping thing that creeps on the earth." So God created man in His [own] image; in the image of God He created him; male and female He created them. Then God blessed them, and God said to them, "Be fruitful and multiply; fill the earth and subdue it; have dominion over the fish of the sea, over the birds of the air, and over every living thing that moves on the earth." (Genesis 1:26-28)

Nowadays, many Christians are uncomfortable with the idea of "ruling," "subduing," or "having dominion." We tend to associate these terms with words like "domination," "oppression," "tyranny," and "exploitation"—and for good reason, because that is exactly how sinful humans have so often perverted our original design. For this reason, when we talk about what it means to be made in God's image, we like to emphasize that this means that every human has incredibly high value, or that we were all made for love, connection, and belonging because God is love. While these things are true, they can distract us from what Genesis shows us here about what it means to be made in the image of God. In this context, it means that we were created to *do what God does*, to work as partners and representatives in His family business.

The first chapter of Genesis lays out the initial pattern for how God "rules" and "subdues" the earth. In six days, He forms the heavens and fills them with sun, moon, and stars, forms the earth and fills it with plants and animals, and forms the seas and fills them with living creatures. God's work looks like *forming* and *filling*—bringing "formless and empty" chaos into order, and then causing it to flourish with life. Our work is to follow this pattern. Timothy Keller explains:

We are called to stand in for God here in the world, exercising stewardship over the rest of creation in his place as his vice-regents. We share in doing the things that God has done in creation—bringing order out of chaos, creatively building a civilization out of the material of physical and human nature, caring for all that God has made.[9]

In Genesis 2, we see that work even came before marriage. God created Adam, His first apprentice, breathed into his nostrils, and told him to go to work!

> Then the LORD God formed a man from the dust of the ground and breathed into his nostrils the breath of life, and the man became a living being . . . The LORD God took the man and put him in the Garden of Eden to work it and take care of it. (Genesis 2:7, 15, NIV)

Significantly, Adam's first job wasn't to build a temple or write Scriptures or meditate on truth or pray or go on a fast. He was assigned to tend the garden and name the animals—to study and build relationship with creation, learn and call out its design, and care for it, protect it, and cause it to be fruitful. He was to get his hands dirty with work, just as God had gotten His hands dirty when He created Adam from the dust. It was because Adam needed a suitable partner to continue and expand this cultural project that God created Eve and blessed them to

---

9 Keller, *Every Good Endeavor*, 36.

be fruitful and multiply. This is what "taking dominion" looked like—Adam and Eve partnering with God, each other, and their growing family, to bring everything into ever-increasing levels of beauty, fruitfulness, flourishing, and delight.

Clearly, before sin entered the world, the Garden of Eden was not a place where humans sat around doing nothing but a place where they were completely blessed and thriving as they worked as apprentices under the Master Craftsman to bring creation into divine order. This is the picture of what God originally designed work to be, and unless we see that picture clearly, we won't understand how the fall affected our work, or how God is restoring us and our work through His great plan of redemption in Christ.

The Curse and the Cross

Work is not a curse—but it did become cursed through sin. The essence of all sin is the rejection of God as our boss and partner and the attempt to rule apart from Him. This is what Adam and Eve did when they listened to the serpent and took the fruit. Instead of firing them and starting over with new apprentices, however, God kept them in place as His image-bearers, for reasons that become apparent by the end of the Bible. He did so first because of the value He placed on His relationship with us, even when we rejected relationship with Him. He had created us not just to be His employees but also His family members and partners. Second, He always had a plan in place to redeem and restore us. But, in His infinite wisdom and patience, this plan involved allowing His rebellious apprentices to have their way and try to do the work He had given them on their own terms. As He told Adam and Eve, this was bound to cause a lot of problems:

To the woman He said:

"I will greatly multiply your sorrow and your conception;
In pain you shall bring forth children;
Your desire [shall be] for your husband,
And he shall rule over you."

Then to Adam He said, "Because you have heeded the voice of your wife, and have eaten from the tree of which I commanded you, saying, 'You shall not eat of it':

"Cursed [is] the ground for your sake;
In toil you shall eat [of] it
All the days of your life.
Both thorns and thistles it shall bring forth for you,
And you shall eat the herb of the field.
In the sweat of your face you shall eat bread
Till you return to the ground,
For out of it you were taken;
For dust you [are],
And to dust you shall return." (Genesis 3:16-19, NKJV)

God was not imposing an arbitrary punishment with these words. He was declaring the natural result of Adam and Eve's choice to run the family business without Him. Fallen humans would continue to work together to raise a family and care for creation, but every aspect of that work and partnership would be full of struggle, frustration, disappointment, and pain.

The effects of the fall still play out in our lives in many ways. First, there are the obvious instances where humans continue to cause blatant harm to one another in professional and personal dealings. Over the years, I've seen people misbehave in just about every way you can think of at work, from the petty to the criminal. I've seen the damage caused when employees decide to lie, cheat, embezzle money, cut corners, and create dissension in the ranks. I've seen employers and business owners get greedy and exploit their organizations for personal advancement. I've seen business partners betray, abuse, viciously sue, and try to destroy each other. On the family side, I've seen lives and families wrecked by affairs, divorce, addiction, and abuse. We all have examples of bad behavior, others' or our own, that have caused destruction in our work and life.

Yet we don't just experience the effects of the fall when people are obviously misbehaving—we also experience them when we're trying our best. Most of the dysfunctional aspects of our work culture that we explored in the last chapter belong in this category. Many of us aspire to good things that are part of God's original design for us—to use our gifts for good, to change the world for the better, to succeed in doing something significant. Yet as we pursue those good things, we struggle and stumble and get disappointed. We make costly mistakes. Circumstances work against us. We put in the effort but don't get the result we hoped for. And even when we do succeed, something's missing. Though the gifts of creativity and intelligence and ingenuity God put in us as His image-bearers shine through in beautiful ways, they can't satisfy us like we want them to. That's what God promised Adam, after all—that he would put the work in but would get "thorns and thistles" in return.

Again, God had a redemptive purpose in allowing the fall. Like the father in the parable of the prodigal son, He let us take our inheritance and taste the pain, disappointment, and meaninglessness of life without Him—not so that we would destroy ourselves, but so that we would come to our senses, see what we're missing, and come home to Him. And unlike the brother in the parable, Jesus, our elder brother, willingly came after us to bring us to our senses, show us what we're missing, and lead us home.

The story of the gospel is not just that Jesus died for our sins so we could be forgiven. It's that through His life, death, and resurrection, Jesus reconciled us to the Father and brought us back into full apprenticeship to Him. The apostle Paul describes Jesus as the "last Adam," meaning that He is the prototype and origin point for a new race of humans who would succeed where the first Adam failed to live and work from complete trust and intimate partnership with God as we were originally designed. Through His ministry, Jesus demonstrated what a faithful apprentice of the Father looks like and told us explicitly that was what He was doing:

> My Father is always at his work to this very day, and I too am working . . . Very truly I tell you, the Son can do nothing by himself; he can do only what he sees his Father doing, because whatever the Father does the Son also does. For the Father loves the Son and shows him all he does. (John 5:17-20, NIV)

Three things stand out strongly in the way Jesus did "the Father's business." The first is His character, work ethic, and lifestyle. Jesus modeled what it looks like for humans to live in deep connection with the Father, totally free from sin, fear, and shame. Because of this connection, Jesus was absolutely secure in His identity, crystal clear on His purpose, and passionately committed to His mission. He spoke and acted with confident authority. He refused to cave to temptation or intimidation that could throw Him into frantic striving and competition or lazy complacency. Instead, He sustained a masterful, wise rhythm and balance of hard work and deep rest. This lifestyle is the "easy yoke" He calls every one of His apprentices—us—to share with Him.

The second thing that stands out to me is that Jesus had two careers. His first career was working for His earthly father, Joseph, as a carpenter, stonemason, or builder. He was a craftsman fulfilling our original cultural mandate to work creatively with the raw materials of Earth and make things that contribute to human flourishing. Jesus used His time doing that work to pray and study the Scriptures in preparation for His second career as a rabbi and prophet. In that career, He chose apprentices (disciples) to join Him in the work of proclaiming and demonstrating the message that the kingdom of God was at hand. The whole thrust of that message was that humans now had access to what Adam and Eve had lost in the garden—relationship with the Father—and that being restored to this relationship would begin to unravel the effects of the curse. Signs of this restoration followed Jesus wherever He went—miraculous feasts, healed bodies, repentant sinners, and corpses raised from death.

As apprentices of Jesus, I think we are to follow this pattern of seeing our calling and career as dual or two-dimensional. We are called to walk in relationship with the Father, Son, and Holy Spirit, discover and develop our unique gifts and abilities, and partner with Him to restore the world and cause it to flourish. And we are to participate in the work of "making disciples" by inviting people to join us as fellow apprentices to Jesus, both through our words and also through our example of apprenticeship. These dimensions are not to be split or compartmentalized in our lives, however, but integrated seamlessly together as they were for Jesus. Jesus did not have a "secular" job as a carpenter and then go into full-time ministry. Whether He was building tables, teaching on a mountain, blessing children, or raising the dead, it was all ministry—service—to God and humanity. And He calls us to the same life of ministry.

The third and final thing we see in the life and work Jesus modeled for us is that they still involved "thorns and thistles"—difficulty, pain, frustration, and fruitlessness. Some people mistakenly believe that because Jesus redeemed us from the curse, we shouldn't have to deal with its effects anymore. They imagine that if they're living the Christian life the way it is supposed to be lived, then they can avoid experiencing resistance, pain, struggle, frustration, and disappointment. I'm not sure where they get this idea, because it shows up nowhere in the Bible. Jesus and the apostles experienced pain, struggle, and suffering, and every generation of humanity will experience the same until Jesus returns to bring about the full and final consummation of heaven and Earth.

Just as the Father had a redemptive purpose in allowing us to walk away and taste the devastation of a life estranged from Him, so too He has a redemptive purpose in allowing us to relearn to walk with Him and partner with Him in cleaning up the mess we have made of the world. This means that what we can expect from the Christian life is not one free of pain and struggle, but one where these experiences are constantly being redeemed and used to bring us to maturity as apprentices who live and work like Jesus.

One of the main reasons people like Nick, Katrina, and Victor inspire and impress me so much is that I see them living this mature, integrated life of apprenticeship to Jesus. You don't have to spend much time with these men and women to recognize that they walk with Jesus. They live with a posture of leaning into His voice and following His Spirit in every department of their lives. Their lives are not split into sacred and secular. They aren't one person at home, one person at church, and one person at work. Their extreme clarity, focus, and mission keep them from being distracted by the world's culture of hustling to look successful on social media, accumulate material wealth, rack up accomplishments, and compete for slots at the top. Neither do they succumb to pressure to keep up some kind of "spiritual hustle" to look more successful in the eyes of the religious community. In everything, they work with high levels of excellence, humility, confidence, and passion. It's extremely attractive and compelling. In so many ways, they show us what the abundant life of apprenticeship to Jesus can and should look like. In the chapters ahead, we'll explore ways for us to grow in living this abundant life for ourselves.

"Life is never made unbearable by circumstances, but only by lack of meaning and purpose."

Victor Frankl
Holocaust survivor, neurologist, psychologist, author

CHAPTER 4

The Journey
of Purpose

Some time ago, a young man named Kendrick asked to talk to me about his frustrations with his job. When we met up for coffee, he launched into a list of complaints about the company where he'd been working for over a year. He said that the culture was unhealthy and full of fear, and turnover was high as a result. Not wanting to be a quitter, Kendrick had put his head down, done his best to tune out the atmosphere of gossip and intimidation, and focused on working hard in hopes that it would be appreciated and rewarded. But the type of work he was doing was repetitive and tedious, and his managers never thanked him or explained how his job was contributing to the company's success. Over time, he had come to feel like a robot, performing his tasks without any excitement or inspiration.

"It's become such a drag to go to work every day," he sighed. "As I'm driving there, all I can think about is that I hope I'm not still doing this when I'm thirty. I don't feel like I'm accomplishing anything. I've been starting to ask myself why I'm giving this company so much when they don't appreciate me. Should I really be working so hard for this?"

I told Kendrick that I understood—a lot of people feel like this about their work, in large part because many companies do not help their employees understand and connect to an inspiring purpose for their jobs. In 2009, Simon Sinek made waves with his bestselling book, *Start with Why*, in which he made the simple argument that most companies try to manipulate people with rewards and punishments rather than inspiring them with great purpose—a clear WHY. He claimed that companies that could clearly identify their purpose and align their culture, strategy, and tactics (the WHAT and HOW) around this purpose would be most effective in inspiring their teams and winning the loyalty of their customers.

But then I went on to challenge Kendrick that just because his company had a purpose deficit didn't mean *he* needed to have a purpose deficit. I began to ask him questions about who he was and what he felt called to do in life. It was then that we started to uncover the real problem. Kendrick hadn't thought deeply about his purpose in life, much less worked to clarify what it was. I encouraged him to work on solving that problem first. "When you have more clarity of purpose, then you'll quickly see where this job aligns or doesn't align with that purpose and you'll be able to see what adjustments you need to make. Maybe you'll gain new perspective on what you're doing every day that will make it more inspiring and fulfilling. Maybe you'll see new ways to do what you do, connect and collaborate better with your peers and superiors, or grow into a new position in your company. Or maybe you'll see that it's time to move on and find another job. If that's the case, clarifying your purpose will help you find a job that fits you better."

Designed to Be Purpose-Driven

Like Kendrick, many people today, believers included, simply do not have deep clarity around what their life is all about. Lacking a strong sense of calling or mission in their work or life's pursuits, they "try on" different purposes, chasing the next job, relationship, experience, or achievement in hopes that it will finally fulfill them, only to find it disappointing and meaningless. When things get difficult or frustrating, they are quick to wonder if they are in the wrong job, career, marriage, city, church, or friend group and look for a way out. Even though many seem to be "successful" by the world's standards, inside they're still hustling and living in survival mode.

People who do have clarity of purpose stand out from the crowd. When I consider the people I know who are "winning at life"—thriving and not just surviving—the primary thing they share in common is their sense of purpose and mission. They just seem to be more secure and confident in who they are. They are better at saying yes and no to things and following through with them. Instead of momentary passion that waxes and wanes with their feelings, they have an internal drive that compels them through tension, discomfort, frustration, pain, and failure. They also seem to be able to find meaning even in the most mundane or humble tasks in life.

There is no doubt that God designed us to live and work with great purpose, and that the more we can discover and live into our true purpose, the more we will thrive. Just understanding the two principles we explored in the last chapter—that everything is spiritual and sacred, and that God created and called us to be His apprentices—will put us miles ahead in this discovery process. These principles show us that God has a great purpose for the human race, and that each of us has an individual purpose that connects to that great purpose. This is why we naturally hunger to be part of something greater than ourselves.

The idea that everything is spiritual and sacred affirms that God cares about and calls people to every type of work in every sector, field, and discipline, because that will bring humans and the world into their potential and place of flourishing. While society tells us that certain jobs are better than others, God places great value and purpose on every kind and stage of work, whether paid or unpaid, entry or executive level, blue collar or white collar, in the home or out of the home. No matter what we are working on, it is connected to divine purpose.

The idea that God created us to be His apprentices and partners in ruling the earth, and that He would pay the greatest price to restore us to that relationship and role, tells us that whatever we're doing is designed to be done *with* Him and to express His kingdom. The desire to do something meaningful, something that changes the world for the better, is not grandiose. It is what we are made for. We each have a unique and important role to play in God's mission to creatively restore people and the world.

Again, seeing the big picture of God's purpose and value for all of us is critical when it comes to understanding our individual purpose. Without being grounded in this appreciation for every one of us doing the job He made us for, we will inevitably struggle with things like comparing ourselves to others, feeling inferior, dishonoring those who do jobs we don't value, or thinking that our job or career is all about us.

Cultivating this appreciation, however, frees us to focus fully on discovering and developing who we were created to be and what we were created to do.

Relationship and Experience

I'm not sure why some of us, like Nick and Katrina, seem to know at an early age what we want and are supposed to do with our lives, while for others of us, it takes a little more time and experimentation to gain clarity on these things. What I do know is that God is intimately involved in each of our journeys and will get us where we need to be if we trust Him. I also know that every one of us will experience plenty of mystery on our journey to discover and live out our purpose, because that's the nature of being apprentices.

As apprentices of Jesus, our first calling is not to do a job but to be with Him and learn from Him. When Jesus called His disciples, He didn't give them a syllabus and itinerary for their three-year mission together. He said, "Follow Me." He insisted that their relationship be built on a certain kind of trust—trust that He was the master who knew more about them and the work He was training them to do than they did, and that He would faithfully guide them into the lessons and experiences they needed to grow.

This means that the most important way for you to discover and connect with your individual purpose is to discover and connect to the Father, Son, and Holy Spirit. Who knows the purpose of a work of art or a great invention better than the one who conceived it and brought it into being? No one knows you more intimately than the One who created you. He is always speaking, and if you will position your heart to listen, you will hear Him speaking to you—through His Word, His still small voice, prophetic words, and many other ways He speaks—about the great purpose for which He made you.

But God doesn't just want to speak to you and tell you your purpose; He wants to *work with you to reveal your purpose*. Consider how He worked with Adam in the garden. He didn't come to Adam and say, "Adam, you need a helper in the work I've called you to do. So here's the plan: I'm going to bring all the animals to you, and you're going to study them and give them names. Through that process, you're going to learn a ton about the world I created you to rule with me—*and* you're going to see that none of these creatures was made specifically to walk by your side. This is going to prepare your heart to be so overjoyed and fulfilled when I finally bring your partner and mate, Eve, to you." God didn't give His apprentice a lecture full of information; He led him into an experience that brought *revelation*. This is how we were created to learn and grow—through relationship and experience.

Significantly, this is how parents teach and train their children. Some lessons come through verbal instruction, but many of the most important lessons come through modeling and exposing kids to various experiences. For example, someone recently asked me, "How did you and Lauren teach your kids work ethic?" My immediate answer was, "We didn't." That is, we didn't teach them explicitly but implicitly. I honestly can't remember one time when Lauren and I sat down with our kids and lectured them on the importance of having a good work ethic. It was simply the culture of our home. I usually left for the office early in the morning and came home, when I turned my attention to helping Lauren with whatever needed doing around the house—making food, assisting with homework, taking kids to sports practice, etc. Lauren always had a number of work, ministry, and house projects she was managing. When the kids got older, I occasionally let them know when things were difficult and overwhelming at the office, but I usually didn't complain or say things like, "I hate my job." Every day, our kids saw us working hard, with a sense of purpose and responsibility, and often with joy. Then, with our support, they tackled the growing levels of responsibility for their chores, schoolwork, sports, and other activities with which we entrusted them. When they encountered difficulties, we helped them figure out how to persevere until they found the solution. That's basically how they developed their work ethic.

In my own life, God revealed my purpose over time in both implicit and explicit ways. I discovered painting serendipitously (or providentially) at eighteen when I found myself stuck at my Uncle Lew's recovering from knee surgery at the same time he had a painter working in the house. There was something captivating about watching this man work. Nowadays we have entire TV networks dedicated to house makeovers, but for me, it was a revelation to discover how enjoyable and satisfying it could be to watch someone transform a living space by swinging a brush. *I could do that,* I thought. This interest led to my first job.

That same year, I attended a church meeting in which an older gentleman called me over and asked if he could give me a prophetic word.

"God says you're called to become a philanthropist," he said.

At the time, I had no idea what the word "philanthropist" meant, and apparently he could see this on my face, because he then asked, "Do you know what a philanthropist is?"

"No."

"It's someone who loves to give away money." He then proceeded to describe the kinds of things a philanthropist does with their money and gave me a few pieces of advice on how to build a long-term plan for financial growth and practicing generosity along the way.

These two experiences—stumbling upon an interest that turned out to be a job I liked and could do well, and receiving a prophetic word— pointed me toward my purpose. However, neither experience equipped me with some kind of roadmap for understanding my purpose and how to fulfill it. Instead, my understanding of my purpose continued to grow and develop as I walked with the Lord and did my best to pursue and steward the opportunities and responsibilities He had given me. In the early years of my career, I understood that my purpose was to do all I could to build a successful business and make a living to support my growing family. As my company and children grew, this purpose expanded as I took on new responsibilities and challenges as a leader, husband, and father. In the last ten years, both my company and children have reached maturity, which has enabled me to venture into new opportunities as a speaker, author, and consultant. Through all of that, I have carried the same core values of honor and generosity. Though I wouldn't class myself as a philanthropist along the lines of Warren Buffet or Bill Gates, I can say that from the beginning of my career till now, giving has been a cornerstone practice in our life, marriage, family, and business. Whether it's swinging a paintbrush, providing jobs for my team and employees, going on dates with Lauren, doing homework with the kids, meeting with clients, or playing with my grandchildren, Elias and Araya, I love to invest my time, energy, work, and money to benefit and transform people's lives.

Discovering Identity

Granting, then, that our understanding of our purpose is something that will grow through both information and revelation over our lifetimes as we walk with the Lord, there are also plenty of tools and insights we can learn from others about the journey to discover our purpose. For instance, Brad Lomenick, founder of the Catalyst leadership conference, offers a helpful concept for understanding our individual purpose and how we live it out in his book *H3 Leadership*. He explains that our purpose—he equates this with the term "calling"—is rooted in our *identity* and expressed through various *assignments* over the course of our lives. If we get these things confused, he argues, it causes problems. For example, if we confuse our calling or assignment with our identity—if we think that what we do is who we are—then we will feel insecure whenever we are not hitting it out of the park doing that thing. Or, if we confuse our calling with our assignment, we will cling to a certain role or job instead of recognizing when it has come to its proper end and transitioning to the next job.

Here is Lomenick's breakdown of this concept[10]:

IDENTITY	CALLING	ASSIGNMENT
Who you are	What you were designed to do best	Where you live out your calling
Does not change	Can change somewhat	Changes, probably many times
The drive	The direction	The destination

The first thing I like about this identity-calling-assignment concept is that it shows us exactly where to start digging deeper to understand

---

10 Brad Lomenick, *H3 Leadership* (New York, NY: HarperCollins Leadership), Kindle edition, 56.

our purpose: our identity. Those of us who, like Kendrick, struggle with a purpose deficit most likely are also struggling to know and be secure in who we are. We still need to discover the unchanging essence of our being.

Consider how most of us respond when someone asks us, "Who are you?" Typically, we give our names, along with some information about the people and place to which we belong or what we do for a living. If the conversation gets more personal, we may share insights about our personality, interests, abilities, accomplishments, or experiences. This is the default way we ourselves think about our identity. However, while all of these paint a picture of who we are, none of them really gets at the deepest unchanging truth about us.

The Bible has a lot to say about our struggle with identity. Consider what we find out about the topic of identity just in the first fifteen chapters of Genesis. In Genesis 2, God names Adam and then gives him the job of *naming*—assigning identity. The genealogies of Genesis 4-5 show us how fathers continued this tradition of naming, and how family line became another essential part of people's identity. However, because of sin, the identities humans pass on produce legacies of evil, violence, and destruction. God wipes the earth clean with the flood and starts over with Noah, but the same problem emerges. When humans become numerous again, the first thing they want to do is to "make a name for [themselves]" (Genesis 11:4)—that is, to define their own identity on their own terms—by building the city and tower of Babel. After God breaks up this project, He calls one man, Abram, to leave his father, homeland, and name behind—to walk away from his identity. God does this so He can lead Abram to a new land, make him the father of a new family, and give him a new name: Abraham, "father of a multitude." To establish Abraham as His covenant partner, God gives him a new identity as the foundation for that purpose.

This theme of identity carries on throughout the Bible, but these opening chapters lay the foundation of its core message. Since the fall, humans have looked to what the important people in their lives say about them, their family line, and their accomplishments to "name" them—to give them an identity—or enable them to "make a name for themselves"—to create their own identity. But God is inviting us into a story where we leave behind those lesser identities to receive the identity He wants to give us, the identity that will position us as His apprentices and partners. He started that story with Abraham, whose identity defined an entire nation, and it culminated in Christ, whose identity defines the new human race.

The New Testament uses the term "adoption" to help us understand how we come to share in Christ's identity, because adoption is a change in relationship that brings about a change in identity. In Christ, we are adopted as fellow sons and daughters of God. His relational standing before the Father is ours, with all the same access, privileges, and rights. There is no deeper, more unchanging truth about who we are than that we are loved children of God—loved so much that Christ would give His life to restore us to the Father and His family. This truth is more powerful and important than anything people have said (or not said) about us or anything we've accomplished (or not accomplished). It's the only foundation upon which to build a truly secure identity that can remain intact no matter what happens.

In *The Business of Honor*, Danny Silk and I devote an entire chapter to unpacking the transition we must make from our old identity—we call it the orphan identity—to our new identity as loved sons and daughters of God, so I encourage you to read that book if you haven't. But perhaps the most important theme in this transition is that we move from a core belief of unworthiness to worthiness. The gospel teaches us to believe, "No matter what I do or don't do, whether I succeed or fail, I am valuable. I am enough. I am worthy of God's love."

The power of believing in our worthiness can't be overstated, because it is the antidote to shame. This is what Brené Brown discovered in her research on shame and connection. Her guiding theory is that human beings are wired for love, connection, and belonging, and that these are what primarily give purpose and meaning to our lives. She has found that when it comes to meeting this core need, people fall into two categories: those who really struggle to experience love, connection, and belonging, and those who don't. The sole difference between them is their core belief about their worthiness. The people who struggle do so because they believe the message of shame, which is that their flaws and failures make them unworthy of love, connection, and belonging. The second group, whom Brown calls the "wholehearted," believe that *in spite of* their flaws and failures, they are worthy of love, connection, and belonging.

I'm convinced that until we receive the love of God and believe the truth that He has adopted us as His beloved children, we won't be able to fully escape from shame around our identity. We will always struggle with a sense of unworthiness, and this will shape everything in our lives—how and why we work, how we do relationships, how we react to circumstances, who we align ourselves with, and more.

As I shared in *The Business of Honor*, I have been on a long journey to discover and believe in my worthiness and overcome the influence of shame in my life. Looking back, I can point to many cases in which the belief in my unworthiness, which I learned and cultivated growing up, influenced my choices and behavior in damaging ways. For example, in the early years of my company, I had a problem with underbidding for jobs. If a client told me my price was too high, I lowered the price until we won their business but lost money on the job. After a few of these painful experiences, which led to us going into debt and having to lay off employees to stay afloat, I was forced to confront the deeper issues that were leading me to make this mistake. The Lord showed me that I felt compelled to win the business of these clients because of my ego. I wasn't secure in my own identity and worthiness, and I thought making those people happy would make me feel more worthy. The more I got anchored in believing in my worthiness in God, the less I was tempted to look for it from others, and this freed me to say no to jobs that would hurt the company.

Becoming anchored in our identity is so incredibly freeing. When the truth of our worthiness, of being the object of God's love and affection, gets deep in our hearts, it breaks off all the false pressure and anxiety around discovering and living out our calling and assignments. It sets us up to see the world through the eyes of a curious, eager child who wants to discover amazing things and take risks with our Father. It builds great confidence in our ability to grow and learn. In short, knowing that we are worthy, loved children of God naturally leads to the posture of humility and learning I described in chapter 1—the posture that attracts wisdom.

Sons and Daughters, Stewards, and Servants

Many years ago, I had an employee who taught me an unforgettable lesson about the benefit we bring to those around us when we are secure enough in our identity to take big risks. Our company once had a job that required us to paint close to two thousand doors. At that time, our standard method was to paint one door at a time, which was very inefficient. Then one day, one of our foremen came to me and said, "I have an idea. I want to go into the underground garage, clean the floors, and set up a shop where we can spray multiple doors at a time like an assembly line."

It was a risky plan—if it didn't work, we were looking at a significant loss of time, labor, and materials. We had never done anything like it before. But my foreman continued to urge the plan and explain why it would work. Eventually I agreed to let him set up the spray shop and paint fifty doors. When he was done, we ran the numbers and saw that he had succeeded in cutting the labor time in half. His innovation didn't just save us on that project; it established a new way for us to paint doors moving forward.

That experience forever impressed me with how powerful it is when just one employee shows up to work, has the curiosity to pay attention and look for different ways to do things better, and has the confidence to bring those ideas to the table. This man was not trying to win brownie points, climb the ladder, or do anything selfish. He was willing to risk having his idea be criticized and turned down. He was truly doing it because he wanted to help us excel in our work. He was serving us. And he did that because he was secure in who he was.

There are two passages of Scripture that tie these elements of secure identity, confident risk-taking, and serving together. The first is Jesus' parable of the talents. A wealthy man entrusts three of his best workers with different sums of money, "each according to his ability" (Matthew 25:15). The first two "put [their] money to work" (25:16) and double it by the time the wealthy man returns, but the third buries his money out of fear. When the man calls his workers to give an account for what they did with his money, he rewards the first two for investing and working with what he gave them, but strongly rebukes the third for his refusal to follow their example.

As loved sons and daughters of the Father, our great purpose is to steward the resources and opportunities He has given to us, and every one of our assignments is to be an expression of serving Him well. This parable shows us that being faithful stewards and effective servants requires *great risk* and *hard work*. The reason the first two workers succeeded in their calling and assignment was because they were secure in their identity and relationship with their boss. They understood that he knew exactly what they could handle and expected them to use what he had given them. This gave them the courage to put the work in and take the risks necessary to grow their money in service to him. They actually saw themselves as partners with the wealthy man in his work of growing and enriching his estate. When the wealthy man saw their heart of loyalty and sacrifice, he knew he had found those whom he could trust with even more—he wanted to share all he had with them!

The third worker, however, saw the wealthy man not as a partner who wanted to be generous with his workers but as "a hard man" (Matthew 25:24). His insecurity shut down his courage to take risks and go to work with the resources and opportunities entrusted to him, and it did not end well for him. In fact, the third worker's fate in this parable implies that there is really only one way to truly fail in life, and that is simply *not to use* the resources and opportunities the Father has given us because of fear and insecurity. Mistakes, losses, disappointment—none of these matter in the long run if we keep choosing to trust the Father and work with what He's given us to the best of our ability.

The other Scripture that pulls our identity (sons and daughters), calling (stewarding), and assignment (serving) together is Philippians 2:3-8, which I consider one of my "life verses":

> Do nothing out of selfish ambition or vain conceit. Rather, in humility value others above yourselves, not looking to your own interests but each of you to the interests of the others. In your relationships with one another, have the same mindset as Christ Jesus: Who, being in very nature God, did not consider equality with God something to be used to his own advantage; rather, he made himself nothing by taking the very nature of a servant, being made in human likeness. And being found in appearance as a man, he humbled himself by becoming obedient to death—even death on a cross! (NIV)

Jesus set the example for what the Father's true sons and daughters are like. In Him we see that being confident in our worthiness should never lead to an attitude of entitlement or self-serving. Rather, it should lead us to understand that we have been given the Father's name and access to the incredible wealth of His love, presence, resources, and opportunities so that we can represent His name and His heart well. We are to steward all of that incredible wealth by imitating Jesus in taking the posture of servants and looking to the interests of others above our own.

Our calling as stewards and assignments to serve should humble us as well as excite us. We all have a steep journey of growth and maturity ahead of us, but we can be confident that our Father will be with us every step of the way, delighting in us as we learn. We will fail and make plenty of mistakes on that journey, but we don't have to be afraid that these can do anything to change our worthiness. In fact, the more shame is removed from our identity, the more we see how our Father can turn our mistakes and failures into rich ground for our transformation and growth, which only deepens our connection and partnership with Him. As long as we are committed to using and cultivating the gifts we've been given, we will succeed.

"You have to be burning with an idea, or a problem, or a wrong that you want to right. If you're not passionate enough from the start, you'll never stick it out."

Steve Jobs, founder of Apple

CHAPTER 5

Do You Deserve Passion?

When I reached out to Nick to ask if I could feature him in this book, I invited him to comment on some of the trends he sees among his peers in the early stages of their careers.

"I have seen a lot of my friends go from job to job to job," he told me. "They do something for a while, but as soon as it's not fun anymore, they say, 'I don't love what I'm doing.' Or my religious friends say, 'This isn't what I'm called to do.' So they decide to do something else. But when I ask them, 'So, what do you love? What are you called to do?' they don't have an answer."

Nick then gave his opinion on why so many of his friends were approaching their careers this way. "I think the fundamental issue comes down to two things. First, people don't know what their purpose is. And because they don't know their purpose, they think they shouldn't be doing something they don't enjoy. I love what I do, but I don't love every part of what I do. But I also know my purpose, so I stick with it. Second, my generation has access to a lot of information, but when we get out into the work world and prove what we actually know, what hard and soft skills we have, we are faced with the reality that we don't know as much as we think. This triggers our pride. We don't want someone to see that we're not as skilled as we say we are. So when a job threatens to do that, we decide it isn't for us."

I thought Nick had put his finger right on one of the biggest wisdom gaps I see people struggling with today—not only people in their twenties, but people of all ages. It seems universal that people want to go to work every day to do something they love, something they are *passionate* about. "Follow your passion" has become a guiding principle for this generation of workers. Unfortunately, however, most of the inspirational speakers who promote this message fail to define what passion even is, much less how to follow it. This leaves people chasing a good feeling, just as Nick said. But feelings are the results of certain beliefs and behaviors. Unless we understand and cultivate the beliefs and behaviors that lead to feelings of passion, we are just setting ourselves up for frustration and disappointment.

The True Meaning of Passion

What is passion? The Oxford American Dictionary defines passion as "strong and barely controllable emotion" and "an intense desire or enthusiasm for something." However, the original meaning of this word may surprise you:

> *passion* (n.) c. 1200, "the sufferings of Christ on the Cross; the death of Christ," from Old French *passion*

"Christ's passion, physical suffering" (10c.), from Late Latin *passionem* (nominative *passio*) "suffering, enduring," from past-participle stem of Latin *pati* "to endure, undergo, experience," a word of uncertain origin. The notion is "that which must be endured." The sense was extended to the sufferings of martyrs, and suffering and pain generally, by early 13c.[11]

The word "passion" is rooted in the story of the gospel! This word originally referred to everything Jesus endured in His most difficult assignment—going to the cross—to fulfill His great calling to save the world. No other Scripture captures this original meaning like Hebrews 12:1-2:

> Therefore, since we are surrounded by such a great cloud of witnesses, let us throw off everything that hinders and the sin that so easily entangles. And let us run with *perseverance* the race marked out for us, fixing our eyes on Jesus, the pioneer and perfecter of faith. For the *joy* set before him he *endured* the cross, scorning its shame, and sat down at the right hand of the throne of God. Consider him who *endured* such opposition from sinners, so that you will not grow weary and lose heart. (NIV, emphasis added)

Jesus pioneered the path of passion for every one of us. Passion

11 https://www.etymonline.com/word/passion#etymonline_v_7291

is far more than a feeling; it is something we do in order to achieve a great, joyful purpose. And what we do is usually the opposite of having a *good* feeling. We endure discomfort and pain because that is what lies between us and our purpose. Specifically, we endure discomfort and pain as essential elements of discipline, training, and instruction in our apprenticeship to God and the work He has given us to do, as the writer of Hebrews goes on to explain:

> Fully embrace God's correction as part of your *training*, for he is doing what any loving father does for his children. For who has ever heard of a child who never had to be corrected? We all should welcome God's *discipline* as the validation of authentic sonship. For if we have never once endured his correction it only proves we are strangers and not sons . . . Now all discipline seems to be more pain than pleasure at the time, yet later it will produce a transformation of character, bringing a harvest of righteousness and peace to those who yield to it. (Hebrews 12:7-8, 11, TPT, emphasis added)

This is one of those Scriptures that can make us uncomfortable just reading it. Until we have actually walked through a genuine experience of the Father bringing correction to our lives—which always brings us into greater healing and freedom and deepens our awareness of His love for us—we will naturally be turned off by the idea of His discipline. But Hebrews 12 is inviting us to discover not just how passion and discipline work in our spiritual growth and formation but also how they work in every area of our lives where we are called to learn, train, grow, and achieve a level of skill, competence, or mastery. Any genuine area of passion in our lives, whether it be a career, a relationship, a hobby, getting in shape, or volunteering for a cause, is going to require hard work, training, and discipline if we hope to be successful enough at it to enjoy its rewards. Put the other way round, all genuine joy and fulfillment we hope to experience in our lives lie on the other side of sacrifice. There is no shortcut around sacrifice if we want passion!

Understanding the true, biblical meaning of passion should lead us to ask very different questions about our work than the ones we ask when we're following the world's script of "follow your passion." The question of whether we are enjoying what we do every day should become much less important. Instead, we should be asking things like, "What is the great, joyful purpose of my life? What am I willing to put the work in to do well? What will I choose to give my life for?"

At the same time, we should be asking, "What are the lessons I am being invited to learn right now? What opportunities and assignments has the Father given me to train me for what's ahead?" I believe each one of us has a "race marked out for us"—a course of assignments carefully designed by God to help us discover and develop the character and skills we need to fulfill our calling. As we saw in the previous chapter, our job as sons and daughters, stewards, and servants is to take what He has put in our hands and use it faithfully, trusting that doing so will lead to growth, increase, and joy. But when we are chasing passionate feelings, we are almost guaranteed to ignore or dismiss the assignments that are actually part of our own passion journey.

Passion Is Something You Earn

The biblical view of passion clarifies something important about our identity, purpose, and assignments, and that is *what we can and can't earn*. Our identity is something we can't earn. It's bestowed on us as a gift. There is nothing we can do to earn our Father's love or change our fundamental worthiness as His sons and daughters. However, the joy of fulfilling our purpose is something we *can and do* earn by doing our assignments.

When people who are in the early years of their career come to me and tell me they just don't feel passionate about the work they're doing every day, what I want to tell them is, "I'm sorry, but you don't deserve to feel passion yet." Knowing this could easily trigger an "Okay, Boomer" eye roll, followed by them completely tuning me out, I instead ask questions that will hopefully help them start to reframe their work in light of their purpose. "What are your long-term goals? What do you want to be doing in your career in ten years? How is what you are doing right now setting you up to get there?" I try to nudge them toward discovering, as Nick said, that they don't have to love every part of their job if they know their purpose. Purpose anchors us into a deeper level of motivation than our feelings. People deeply connected to their purpose will do it no matter how it makes them feel. I also want to nudge them toward the biblical definition of passion as a great, joyful purpose we endure discipline to achieve. Do we deserve to be passionate about our work? We do if we earn it.

I'm not the only one who believes this to be true. In his book *Drive*, Daniel Pink summarized the current research on what makes work intrinsically rewarding—that is, what causes work itself to give us a sense of fulfillment, satisfaction, and joy that motivates us to keep doing it— and said it came down to three main factors: autonomy, mastery, and purpose. Basically, we enjoy work more the more we have *control* over what, how, when, and with whom we work; the more our work involves us reaching levels of *competence* and excellence in certain knowledge and skills; and the more our work is *connected* to a greater mission we care about. In *The Business of Honor*, I devote an entire chapter to why and how honoring businesses, organizations, and teams should build a culture that maximizes these rewards for people. But even if leaders try to create this ideal work environment, the fact remains that people must earn these rewards through hard, focused work.

This is the theme of Cal Newport's book *So Good They Can't Ignore You: Why Skills Trump Passion in the Quest for Work You Love*. Newport begins by making the case for why "follow your passion" is bad advice all around. Most people who end up doing a job they love don't get there by trying to find a job that matches a pre-existing passion in their life, he argues. Rather, they adopt what he calls a "craftsman mindset" toward their work. Instead of asking, "What does the world have to offer me?" (he calls this the "passion mindset"), the craftsman mindset asks, "What do I have to offer the world?" This mindset leads them to do their work in a way that leads to—*earns*—autonomy, mastery, and purpose.

Those who adopt the craftsman mindset focus on mastery first and foremost, Newport explains. They understand that their priority is to get *really good* at a valuable and unique skill or set of skills they can offer the world. The title of his book comes from a quote by comedian Steve Martin. When people asked Martin how to advance in their careers as performers or entertainers, he would say, "Be so good they can't ignore you." And becoming that good at any skill, whether it's singing, writing books, woodworking, fixing cars, raising a child, or running a company, requires the same thing. While innate talents, gifts, and interests can help us discern which skills we ought to focus on, the thing that actually leads to mastery is something the experts call "deliberate practice." Deliberate practice is work that involves three things:

1. Clearly defined goals or standards for the level of skill or knowledge you want to reach,

2. A method of working that consistently pushes you against the limits of your ability so that you're actually uncomfortable, and

3. Immediate, clear feedback on your performance so you can see what you're doing right and wrong and adjust accordingly.

Take physical training for example. If you want to train your body to do a certain skill, you first need clearly defined goals and benchmarks. Do you want to be able to run a marathon or bench press three hundred pounds? Then you need a training regimen that will get you there, and it will involve incremental challenges that will stretch you beyond your current capacity. Last, you need feedback from coaches, mirrors, timers, and anything else that can measure and report on your performance so that you can see what you're doing well and what you need to improve.

How much deliberate practice does it take to become *really good* at something? According to the experts, somewhere around ten thousand hours, or about ten years, of deliberate practice is what it takes most people to reach a high level of mastery or competence in a valuable skill. Malcolm Gladwell calls this "The Ten Thousand Hour Rule."

Putting in your ten thousand hours to achieve mastery is the true meaning of "paying your dues." It's unfortunate that so many people don't understand this at the beginning of their work lives. For many, paying their dues means climbing the ladder of position in a given field, rather than understanding that each position represents a level and set of skills, and that it's mastering those skills that will be most rewarding for them, not reaching a certain position. What is more, if you don't prioritize mastery and somehow end up in a certain position without the level of competence you need to succeed, it could be disastrous.

As Newport points out, many people today go chasing jobs that give them greater levels of autonomy and purpose. They want freedom from their cubicles and the corporate grind. They want to be doing something connected to "social justice." But if they neglect the importance of mastery, their ability to create a viable life as a freelancer or entrepreneur, or to contribute something valuable to a social justice mission, will be greatly limited. If you first earn mastery, then you set yourself up to earn the other intrinsic rewards.

Discovering Passion

My niece, Addie Hamilton, has been learning this truth about craftsmanship and mastery in her career. Addie is a talented and hardworking jazz singer, songwriter, and entertainer who, though still in her early twenties, has already put a ton of work into developing her craft—close to ten thousand hours if not more—and built a solid résumé of work that has been featured in television shows, commercials, and film. When I asked Addie how she discovered her passion for music, she told me it all began when she discovered her grandmother's old jazz records and turntable at the age of fourteen.

"We never really had music playing in our house when I was growing up," she told me. "What we did have was plenty of noise and entertainment. With six siblings and multiple friends over all the time, our house was like a continuous big birthday party. When I found those records, I had never heard any music like that. It was a sharp contrast to hear these calming, organized sounds that made you feel things, and it just stoked my curiosity to try to make that kind of music for myself."

Following her curiosity, Addie began playing around making her own jazz music and, at sixteen years old, attended a jazz intensive in Fullerton, California, led by musicians from the Berklee College of Music. The very first song she collaborated on at the intensive ended up getting picked up by a daytime television show and was nominated for an Emmy. She began to put up original songs on YouTube, which drew interest from a number of music publishers. She knew she had found the area of skill and passion she wanted to pursue as a career.

However, after some of these early successes, Addie began to struggle. She had a very specific vision for the kind of creative work she wanted to do and ended up turning down a number of offers that didn't seem to fit that exact vision. At the same time, however, she wasn't landing the kind of offers she was looking for. Finally, she realized this was not working for her and began saying yes to offers that weren't exactly what she wanted to do in the long term but which were all in her field and industry. As she soon discovered, every offer she took led to other opportunities and offers. Writing a simple commercial jingle led to her collaborating on a horror film. Offering to help with set design, hair, and makeup at an event led to a collaboration with an orchestra.

Now, after four years of doing all kinds of creative jobs for all kinds of projects, Addie sees that she has been building a rich body of knowledge and experience and developing the critical connections and partnerships that will enable her to launch her own creative projects down the road. She is building the mastery she needs to design, write, produce, and perform her own jazz shows. But in the process, she has also discovered something even more important about passion. "No matter what specific job I'm doing or project I'm part of, it's all creative work that's part of telling a story and creating an experience for people. That's where the real joy and passion come from—doing the work."

The Work Behind the Work

Newport's "craftsman mindset" aligns beautifully with the ideas we've been exploring around our original design and calling to be apprentices to the Master Craftsman who built this world and wants us to carry on His work. "What do I have to offer the world?" is absolutely the question we should be asking as sons and daughters called to steward the life our Father has given us and use it to serve Him and others. This question should awaken our curiosity and lead us to discover and unlock the passion found in doing the work we were made for.

Yet many of us today, believers as well as nonbelievers, struggle to accept that we must pay our dues and put in the hard work required for mastery and excellence in our stewardship and service. Why?

Nick's comment about the reason his peers leave jobs gives us a clue to the real issue with work that we all need to address. What makes someone quit a job to avoid having their areas of weakness or lack exposed? Nick called it pride, which it is—but it is also *shame*. When shame is out of the picture, we don't care about admitting that we don't know something or aren't competent in some area yet. In fact, we readily do so because it creates opportunities for us to learn and grow. But when we are looking at our weaknesses through the eyes of shame, we see only opportunities for rejection, ridicule, and punishment. So, we do all we can to avoid them, even at the cost of our relationships, careers, and everything we could eventually call our "passion."

Consider again the demands of deliberate practice—setting clear goals, stretching our limits beyond our comfort zone, and seeking immediate feedback on our performance and progress. If there is any shame lingering in our identities and mindsets around our work, these demands will quickly trigger it. The entire process of deliberate practice is actually designed to expose our weakness and bring us to the point of failure, because that is the nature of a learning and growing process. To return to the earlier example of physical training, reaching the "point of failure" over and over again is a specific goal in most training regimens; because unless you reach that point, the muscles and systems of the body won't be stimulated and required to develop further. Yes, failure is painful. But what really matters is how we choose to respond to that pain. Will we double down on the message of shame, embrace failure as our identity, and give up on the goal of mastery? Or will we recognize failure as a critical part of learning and press forward through it?

The work of dealing with our internal fear and shame is *the work behind the work* God has given us to do. I am convinced that He cares more about this internal work than He does about any particular assignment He gives us, because it is this internal work that shapes our character so that we can actually think and work with passion like He does. I believe one of His primary goals for us as we do our work is to bring issues of the heart to the surface so we can overcome the shame of our old, orphan identity. Besides our core relationships, our work is the place where the Father disciplines us into becoming secure, confident sons and daughters who are capable of embracing the messy, uncomfortable journey required to become excellent at the things He's called us to do.

Overcoming Perfectionism

My friend Allison Armerding is an author collaborator who worked with me on *The Business of Honor* and now this book. In the course of discussing what it means to "do the work behind the work" together, she described some of the ways that God has shaped her character through her work.

Allison has two primary "passions," or areas of interest and skill—writing and music—and earned degrees in both English literature and classical voice performance (opera). Her goal was to pursue a career in opera, but like many performing artists, she discovered after grad school that there was no clear map for achieving this. She ended up spending five years juggling multiple gigs and jobs that were all related to music and writing in some way but didn't ultimately launch her into a career. This difficult season brought deep-seated insecurities in her to the surface.

"I couldn't see it at the time, but the real problem was that I had never really had to push through significant disappointment and failure in my life," Allison told me. "I had always worked hard and succeeded, so when I began to hit repeated setbacks or closed doors, I thought it meant I was a failure. I wish I had known about the craftsman mindset and putting in my ten thousand hours of deliberate practice back then. I think that would have helped me adjust my expectations for myself and help me understand I was still on a learning journey to mastery. Instead, my sense of failure just grew to the point where I wanted to quit everything."

Unexpectedly, it was at her lowest point of feeling like a failure that Allison's freelance writing and editing business, which she had done as a "side hustle" for ten years by this time, began to take off. Putting her head down, she began tackling project after project, and before long she realized that God was inviting her to steward this business as her current full-time assignment. In the process of giving herself to her work, Allison began to face and overcome her fear of failure. She discovered the Enneagram personality typing system and learned that she was a Type One (often called The Perfectionist), which helped her understand where her shame and insecurity were coming from. On the positive side, as a perfectionist, she had always had extremely high standards and expectations for herself and her work, and her commitment to excellence had been key to winning her clients' business. On the negative side, even when she was successful, she never felt she was living up to her own expectations, and her "inner critic" would regularly beat her up with all the ways she was falling short or needed improvement.

Armed with these insights, Allison began making progress in "doing the work behind the work." For her, this has meant practicing the discipline of continuously bringing her expectations and the voice of her inner critic to the Father and asking Him to correct them with His truth. As she has leaned into the Father's voice, which sounds exactly opposite to her inner critic, and become more secure in His expectations for her, she has gotten more and more comfortable embracing the demands of deliberate practice as she pursues mastery as a writer, editor, and author coach. Learning to deal with her inner critic is also helping her recover her love of making music and the joy it brings her when she can share it with others. "Doing the work behind the work" is contributing to her experiencing growing levels of control in how she works, competence in what she delivers to clients, and connection with people and projects she cares about.

Scorning Shame

Jesus told us, "Whoever wants to be my disciple must deny themselves and take up their cross daily and follow me" (Luke 9:23, NIV). Many teachers emphasize that this means we must die to every selfish agenda we have for our lives that doesn't align with Christ's. But I think there's a more positive sense to Jesus' words. He is calling us to get up every day and live the same life of *passion* He lived—the kind of life where we invest, sacrifice, struggle, and endure to achieve the purposes for which He called us.

As Hebrews 12:2 notes, the cross is also the place where we learn to deal with our shame like Jesus did. Jesus "scorned the shame" of the cross. The Greek word for "scorn" means "to think nothing of." In the world's eyes, Jesus on the cross was the ultimate picture of failure and shame—a naked, condemned criminal dying slowly in public. Yet in His own mind and heart, He was finishing the work the Father had given Him to do and was bringing Him glory. This is the same internal freedom, joy, and satisfaction our Father wants to give us as we get up every day and take up the work He has given us to do. And this is the ultimate key to working and living with passion.

"The more you like yourself, the less you are like anyone else, which makes you unique."

Walt Disney

CHAPTER 6

Discovering and Developing Your Unique Design

One of the things I love about the Lord is how specific and surprising He is in designing the assignments through which each of His sons and daughters can discover and fulfill their purpose. For some of us, our assignments can look fairly linear, while for others they can feel pretty random and disconnected until we step back and see the picture He's been putting together. His process may seem messy and full of mystery, but He is the master at turning it into a story full of goodness, truth, and beauty.

For forty years, my primary assignment was growing a family and a business. Now He's added writing, speaking, and consulting to my plate. The thread that connects both assignments is fathering people and helping them grow and transform.

In Katrina's case, He gave her a two-career strategy where her first big assignment was to work in healthcare and raise money for her next big assignment: buying her parents' farm and expanding the family legacy. I see a thread of helping people find healing and wholeness, first through medicine and then through hospitality, linking both assignments.

He gave Nick a vision of being a finance entrepreneur at a young age, which led him to be very focused in his personal investments, college education, internships, exploration, and experimentation leading up to launching his own venture. Nick is still young in his career, but I already see a strong theme of helping people clarify their purpose and build their legacy unfolding in his life.

Victor's first few jobs in banking showed him who he didn't want to be and the culture he didn't want to work in, setting him up to feel the difference when he found the organization and role that aligned with his values and abilities. After two decades in that assignment, he has come to see his calling as being a Joseph who advises kings on how to steward their resources well for the years ahead.

Growing up in a large family developed Addie's comfort interacting with lots of people and her love of entertainment, and her discovery of jazz music at a young age impressed on her the power of music to create a powerful emotional, and even healing, experience in people. Like Nick, she is still in the early years of her career, and her current assignment involves a very diverse plate of work, but through it all she is using her creative gifts to create delightful and healing artistic experiences for people.

Though Allison's career has looked nothing like what she expected after finishing her formal training, all her assignments as a writer, editor, teacher, coach, and performer have grown her skills and helped her find her niche as an author collaborator. Increasingly, she recognizes that she is called to help people clarify and amplify their story, voice, and authority.

Of course, there's much more to each of these individual's stories than these few details, but just a few broad brushstrokes reveal a unique and beautiful pattern. When you commit to working for and with the Lord as a son/daughter, steward, and servant, you can trust Him to lead you on the path to fulfill your unique calling, even when you can't see it in the midst of a particular assignment. This means that if you are clear on what your current assignments are, you can and ought to give yourself fully to them, trusting that God's deeper purpose will emerge at some point in the process. Yes, pursuing a deeper understanding of your identity and purpose, as I have encouraged you to do in the last two chapters, should be an ongoing practice through the various seasons and assignments of your life. However, those are things we often see best from thirty thousand feet—those key moments of reflection, typically during or after a transition from one assignment to the next, where we step back and look at the big picture that has emerged over months and years of stewardship and service in a certain job or role. When it comes to what we get up and do on a daily basis, we should be giving our full attention to our current assignment.

Whatever Your Hand Finds to Do

How can you recognize your current assignment? It's not as complicated as you may think. Your current assignment is simply the complete picture of the resources, opportunities, roles, and relationships for which you are presently responsible. This includes your job or training; your relationship with God, family, friends, coworkers, and community; your money and possessions; and your own physical, emotional, and spiritual health. These are the things God has "put into your hand." The main thing God cares about is that you are fully engaged in the work of stewarding these responsibilities. As the Bible puts it, "Whatever your hand finds to do, do it with all your might" (Ecclesiastes 9:10). And, "Whatever you do, work at it with all your heart, as working for the Lord" (Colossians 3:23). Or one of my favorites: "Make a careful exploration of who you are and the work you have been given, and then sink yourself into that. Don't be impressed with yourself. Don't compare yourself with others. Each of you must take responsibility for doing the creative best you can with your own life" (Galatians 6:4-5, MSG).

Full engagement is required not only to fulfill a particular job, task, or function at our greatest level of excellence but also to learn and grow from the lessons God wants to teach us in our current assignment. His goal in every assignment is to give us wisdom about Himself, ourselves, others, and the work He has given us to do, and form us into mature sons and daughters who represent Him well. And wisdom, as I said in chapter 1, comes largely from experiences that teach us discernment. Discernment means knowing both who we are and who we are not, what we're good at and what we're not good at. It's knowing both how to work and how not to work. It's knowing both how to foster effective collaboration with others and how not to do that. These are the big lessons we need to be giving our whole hearts to learning in every assignment.

To navigate these lessons well, we need to be paying attention to what's comfortable and uncomfortable—and why. Today, so many people are tempted to jump ship on a current job the moment it gets uncomfortable, without trying to understand where that discomfort is coming from and the best way to respond to it. In almost every case, the path to wisdom is not running from discomfort but facing it, understanding it, and identifying the best way to deal with it.

As we saw in the last chapter, discomfort is an essential element of deliberate practice leading to mastery, so we need to build a positive association with pushing through that kind of discomfort. Like weightlifters who come to love feeling sore because they know this means they are building muscles, the goal is to find that sweet spot where our assignments are stretching and challenging us in a satisfying way and producing good results as we give them our full effort. The more we live from that sweet spot, the more we will become uncomfortable with being too comfortable, because it will signal to us that we are not growing.

On the other hand, there's also discomfort that comes because something is wrong, broken, or unhealthy and needs to be adjusted. Sometimes it's because we're doing a role that doesn't fit our personality or gifts. Sometimes it's an approach or technique to work that is ineffective, inefficient, or unsustainable. Sometimes it's dysfunction or a clash in values in the people and culture around us. And sometimes it's an issue with our beliefs, motives, or character. Encountering this kind of discomfort is just as important and valuable as the positive discomfort of hard work and growth! Though often painful, these experiences of struggle, friction, and failure bring things to the surface in us that we need to see, because they will hinder our growth if we don't address them. God wants us to be able to discern these problems accurately and receive His wisdom for how to overcome them so that we can become healthy, strong, and skilled in every area of our lives.

An Unlikely Career Journey

My friend Chris has been on a unique journey to discover his sweet spot in his career. In early 2020, we met up for coffee, where he told me he had just been accepted to a graduate program in theology and wanted my opinion on his decision to complete a PhD and pursue a career in academia.

I'm sure my face registered my surprise at this news. The last I had known was that Christ had been thriving as a manager at a construction company and the owner wanted to groom him to take the company over when he retired. This dramatic pivot into academia seemed like such a left-field move to me.

With my usual frankness, I said, "Chris, I am not really the best person to ask because I have worked in the same job for my entire career. So, this sounds like a crazy idea to me. What brought you to this decision?"

Chris opened up and began to share more details of his career journey with me. From the time he was five years old, his dream was to go to a military service academy and disciple people in the military as his grandfathers, two uncles, and father had all done. However, after graduating from the Naval Academy and joining the Navy, he quickly discovered that the organizational culture largely prevented officers from interacting with enlisted soldiers. Realizing he would never be able to work with people like he wanted, he decided to leave the Navy as early as he could.

Chris next took a teaching job at a Christian school—the school my kids attended, which is where I first met him. As a teacher, he was free to do all the things he'd dreamed of doing in the Navy: teaching, mentoring, coaching, leading student mission trips, getting involved in the chapel program, and building relationships with young people. But over his eight years in that assignment, he came up against another culture problem—the school's approach to discipleship was conservative evangelical, while he embraced a more charismatic, Holy Spirit-focused expression.

So, Chris and his wife transitioned to church ministry, where Chris had the freedom to lead them in the passionate, Holy Spirit-filled discipleship he'd longed to practice at the Christian school. At the same time, Chris encountered yet another culture issue: his church was in the midst of a leadership transition with undefined roles and responsibilities and high levels of uncertainty. After three years of over-performing in reaction to this, he realized he was neglecting his family and on the road to burnout.

His next job with the construction company was a godsend, Chris told me. The company culture gave him clearly defined roles, responsibilities, and healthy boundaries between work and life. As Chris and his wife recovered from the previous season in ministry, they reflected on their journey and prayed about what God might have next for them. Gradually it had become clear that the primary gifting and passion of their family lay in academia, and that they had a sweet spot working with college-aged kids and young adults. Specifically, Chris felt called to teach, which meant he needed a PhD.

Chris figured the best way to see if this was really God's plan for him was to apply for the program that seemed most ideal but also like a long shot. When he got into the prestigious theology program at St. Andrews University in Scotland, he was shocked. It seemed like a sign, but it also meant uprooting their family and moving to the UK for the better part of a decade.

"I talked to a friend and mentor who is president of another school," Chris told me. "And she said something that helped me make the final decision. She told me to ask myself if being accepted in the program was a compliment, a catalyst, or a call. A compliment is nice and reassuring but doesn't change anything. Catalysts can inspire you in a certain direction, but you don't necessarily take those opportunities. A call is straightforward. You shouldn't sacrifice a good job and uproot your family unless it is clearly a call from God. In the end, what convinced me was the knowledge that if I am truly called to disciple people like I believe I am, I must be willing to be discipled myself. Submitting to this academic path is the first step to being able to disciple people in academia."

Hearing Chris's story like this connected the dots for me. "I get it, Chris. It sounds like discipleship and teaching are your family business. You're going into the family business."

Chris looked thoughtful. "I haven't thought about it exactly like that, but you're right."

Keys to Finding Your Sweet Spot

I loved hearing how Chris had come to understand what each of his jobs had contributed to his ability to discern his sweet spot. It especially stood out to me that in each position, he succeeded in certain areas and struggled in others, but *both the success and the struggle* provided him with key insights about what he was called to do and how he was called to do it.

In my experience and observation, there are at least four areas or dimensions that come into play in the process of discovering our sweet spot:

1. Gifts and personality
2. Execution

3. Culture
4. Character

Let's take a look at each of these areas and ways we can grow in discernment through both success and struggle.

Gifts and Personality

Each of us has a unique set of abilities and way of showing up in the world. The more we understand about our gifts and personality, the more we will grow in awareness about what kind of work we should be doing and how to do it effectively.

As Chris's first job in the Navy illustrates, there are certain jobs we simply should not do because they are categorically a bad fit for our personality and gifts. Chris is a highly relational person with a strong teaching gift. An administrative or executive position with restricted relational contact with people was an obvious mismatch with his personality and would not allow him to use his gifts. Though it was probably disappointing to give up his childhood dream of a military career, he was discerning enough to know that he needed to find a role where he could be himself.

When people end up or stay in roles that don't fit their personalities or gifts, it can be very costly, both to them and their teams and organizations. This is a common problem in smaller organizations like churches or startups, where people take on multiple roles and jobs to meet needs and keep things running. For example, I once knew a woman who stepped in to help her husband with his business in its early days. She was capable and hard-working, but as the business grew and became more complex, it became increasingly obvious that many of the things she was handling were not a good fit for her personality and gifts. Unfortunately, she didn't discern this mismatch and spent years trying to adapt to the demands of her role. Over time, this just made her more anxious, frustrated, exhausted, and unable to perform at the necessary level, which in turn created significant stress in both her marriage and the company. In the end, she and her husband hired a consultant who had the tools to help her see that she wasn't the problem; she simply didn't fit the role she was trying to perform. She agreed to step down and find another job that suited her, and her husband was able to fill her place with someone who had the gifts and personality to thrive there. It's not too much to say that these changes saved their marriage and their company.

Personality and gift-typing tools like the DISC profile, Strengthsfinder, Meyers-Briggs, and the Enneagram can be extremely helpful in discerning our sweet spot. They not only help to show us the kind of roles that will suit us, but they also show us how to function in those roles in a healthy way. I have used the DISC profile for years as a tool to help me and my team understand how to communicate and collaborate with each other effectively. I have also started learning more about the Enneagram as it has become more popular, and I appreciate how it emphasizes that we must embrace a path of growth to develop a healthy, integrated personality. As Chris's post-Navy jobs as a teacher, pastor, and project coordinator illustrate, for example, even when we're in a job that does fit our personality and gifts, there is still a fine-tuning process where we must learn to function in a healthy way.

Execution

When we approach our work with a craftsman mindset and focus on putting in our ten thousand hours of deliberate practice, it's appropriate to go through a process of moving from "this is how this work has always been done" to "this is how I am uniquely created to do this work." We begin by conforming to a certain skill, art, or discipline. None of us can achieve mastery without learning the fundamentals and becoming familiar with what other humans have done to advance the particular skill, art, or discipline to its current state. In the process of learning to conform ourselves to the training protocols and best practices of our work, however, we will begin to learn things about ourselves and the work itself that will move us into experimentation, leading to innovation in how we work. This development in execution enables us to achieve personal excellence and make our own unique contribution to the world through our work.

This idea of progressing from conformity to innovation is at least as old as the European medieval guilds. Parents would pay to apprentice their child with a master craftsman at the age of eleven or twelve. The child would live with, serve, and be trained by the master craftsman until he was good enough to be hired on as a journeyman (conformity). He was called a journeyman because the next stage of his training and work involved traveling from city to city and learning from the master craftsmen in various workshops and studios (experimentation). In order to graduate to master craftsman, he had to create a "masterpiece" that demonstrated his ability to produce work that not only met the standards of excellence set by the guild but also distinguished his work as his own (innovation).

In Chris's case, we could say that he started his career by conforming to the model he had grown up with—discipleship in a military context. After years of working with that model at the Christian school, he began to see where this approach was not meeting certain needs in his students and did not align fully with his own beliefs and values. This led him to experiment with a new approach to discipleship during his three years as a pastor. As Chris steps into his next season of training, I believe he will continue to develop his own unique approach to teaching and discipleship.

Many people struggle to achieve true excellence in their work because they falter on their journey from conformity to innovation. Some resist mastering the fundamentals of their craft, art, or discipline. Some achieve a level that is "good enough" and then stop developing for various reasons. Still others fail to innovate because they don't do the work required to integrate and refine what they've learned in the previous stages. However, if you truly want to find your sweet spot, you must commit fully to excellence in execution.

Culture

Culture also plays a significant role in finding our sweet spot. The culture of an organization is built on the practices that honor and protect their core values. Every culture falls somewhere on two continuums: strong vs. weak, and healthy vs. unhealthy. Here's a breakdown:

1. Strong culture: the values are clear and the practices are aligned with them.
2. Weak culture: the values are unclear and the practices don't align with them.
3. Healthy culture: a strong culture with values and practices that cause people to succeed and flourish.
4. Unhealthy culture: either a strong culture with unhealthy values and practices, or a weak culture.

As Chris noted, each of the organizations he worked in had a very different culture. The Navy had a strong culture, but it wasn't healthy, at least for Chris, because it didn't share his core value for relationship. On paper, the Christian school shared his value for relationship and discipleship, but when it came to practice, they weren't aligned with how to express and honor that value. At the church, Chris was free to practice his values to some degree, but the weak culture meant that his work wasn't contributing to or benefitting from any cultural momentum. After three unhealthy cultures, Chris was able to experience a healthy culture fit at the construction company as a project coordinator. In the end, both the unhealthy and healthy cultures have helped Chris to recognize the environment where he will thrive.

As believers, we are all called to bring a healthy culture with us to work, even if our organization doesn't have one. Some of our assignments in unhealthy cultures will be relatively short, as Chris's were. But some of us will have an assignment to stay with a particular organization for a long haul and take on more leadership and responsibility to bring change. Others of us will have an assignment to start our own businesses, teams, or organizations and establish healthy culture in them. Whatever the path the Lord takes us on, we can be sure that He will teach us how to become healthy people whose practices align with our core values so that we can positively influence and impact those around us.

Character

That brings us to character development, that final key element in our journey to find our sweet spot. In Romans, Paul tells us that "suffering produces perseverance; perseverance, character; and character, hope" (Romans 5:3-4, NIV). Character is something that develops in our lives as we are tested and proven to be genuine people of authenticity and integrity, people whose internal and external worlds are fully aligned, and who look more and more like Christ.

God's ultimate purpose in every assignment is to transform us from the inside out. In every one of us, there is a core conflict between the genuine person God created us to be and the wounds, fears, wrong beliefs, and bad habits that will hold us back from growing into that person. As we saw in Allison's story in the last chapter, He uses our work to bring this conflict in our hearts to the surface so we can align our beliefs and motives with His truth.

In Chris's case, his character was shaped in many positive ways by growing up in a family that valued respect for authority, discipline, hard work, and excellence. Yet these character strengths had a weak side. Chris actually grew up hungering for the thing that was often missing in his family culture—warm, authentic relationship with God and others not based on performance. Yet his deference to and desire to please those in authority and his drive to perform, which made him successful in many ways, had the potential to sabotage his own growth into becoming the kind of authentic, relationally healthy leader he wanted to be. Each of his jobs helped to bring this core conflict in Chris's character to the surface and reveal his path of growth—becoming an integrated man, husband, father, teacher, and leader who can work hard with excellence without being hung up by a performance mindset and people-pleasing. Through his journey of work, God has been faithfully forming Chris into a relationally authentic disciple who can disciple others in the same way.

Without learning to discern God's purpose for our character development, we'll never really be able to experience alignment and integrity in our identity, purpose, and assignments. One of my friend Danny

Silk's favorite sayings is, "Wherever you go, there you are." Many people today leave jobs because they think the discomfort they're feeling is due to some breakdown or friction in the areas of gifts and personality, execution, or culture. But often the real issue is rooted much more deeply in the core beliefs and motives of their heart. This is why they move on to the next job and find the same problems cropping up for them. They brought themselves with them. In contrast, when we lean into the discomfort and ask God what He may be wanting to deal with in our hearts, we position ourselves for personal transformation. When God moves us to our next assignment, we will take a wiser, healthier person with us.

Reflect

Take a moment to think about your current assignment.

- What are you learning about your personality and gifts in your current role?
- Do you know where you are in your journey of execution—conformity, experimentation, or innovation?
- How would you describe the culture of your workplace—strong, weak, healthy, unhealthy?
- What is God showing you about your character?

The more you learn to pay attention to these things, the more you will grow in your ability to discern and apply wisdom as you discover and develop into the person, apprentice, and worker you were uniquely designed to be.

"My business grew on my understanding that customers are always looking for somebody who is dependable and polite and will take care of them."

Truett Cathy, founder of Chick-fil-A

CHAPTER 7

Passion Is Connected to People

My friends Jimmy and Genea Horner are the directors of a nonprofit called The Mission, which has orphanages in Mexico, Romania, and Nicaragua. Lauren and I have visited their base in Tijuana, Mexico, on multiple occasions, and during one of these visits, Jimmy introduced me to their base manager, a woman named Karina. After making small talk for a few minutes, I jokingly asked Karina, "So, how long have you been putting up with Jimmy?"

Karina laughed and said, "Oh, about twenty-five years."

At first, I thought she was joking back at me, because she didn't look a day over thirty. Then I realized that she was being serious. "Twenty-five years? How is that possible?"

Karina explained that she and her four younger siblings had come to live at the orphanage when she was eight years old. She grew up on the base, went to school there, started working for the organization in high school, and eventually worked her way up to base manager.

I was astonished by this story and wanted to know more. "Tell me, Karina—why did you stay?"

"Well, the Horners and the kids I grew up with here became my family," Karina said. "I have never even considered leaving."

After Karina left, Jimmy and Genea filled me in on more of her story. Like many of the orphans at The Mission, Karina's early childhood had been marked by tragic loss. Her mother had been dying of cancer when she brought Karina and her siblings to the orphanage, having no one else to care for them after she was gone. At her mother's funeral, Karina had told the Lord that she would serve Him if He took care of her and her siblings. Her prayer was answered when Jimmy's parents, Steve and Cathy Horner, who originally founded The Mission and were running it at that time, adopted Karina and her siblings. When she was sixteen, Jimmy and Genea invited her to move out of the larger orphanage facility to live with their immediate family, where she grew even closer to them and helped them raise their kids.

Karina, like the rest of the Horner family, had worked for Steve and Cathy from her teenage years on, traveling with them throughout Mexico and helping to build churches, youth centers, and elementary schools. By the time Jimmy and Genea asked her to manage the Tijuana base, she knew the ministry inside and out. They had trained her in the areas where she lacked experience, encouraged her to ask lots of questions, allowed her to navigate difficult situations and make tough decisions, and walked alongside her through it all so she could be successful.

"I think Karina has impacted us more than we've impacted her," Genea told me. "We even named one of our daughters after her. She carries the heart of The Mission like no one else—to see an orphanless world where *no one* knows what it's like to be without family. We define family as something you choose—not something determined by blood or an adoption certificate. Karina has chosen family from the beginning, and over and over again. She is deeply loyal, hard-working, wise, slow to decide, quick to protect, and passionate about building a team that is also loyal, hard-working, and co-labors as a family."

Lauren and I ended up staying on base for a week, and I got to see Karina in action. If I hadn't heard her story, I would have just been impressed by her joy, work ethic, skill, and efficiency in keeping the base running smoothly. But knowing she had grown up there made watching her even more impactful for me. Her work was an expression of so many things. It was certainly evidence that the Horners were doing great work and bearing excellent, long-lasting fruit in the kids they had poured themselves into for decades. It was a beautiful expression of the gospel in action, the power of the love of Jesus to transform orphans into sons and daughters. It was also an amazing example of apprenticeship leading to mastery. Karina had faithfully sat under and served the Horners, then put her training and experience to work as an empowered leader serving alongside them. Like Chris, Karina had gone into the family business. The love she had received, which had transformed her life, was now the love she lived to give away.

This is how it's supposed to be, I thought. It wasn't that I thought every orphan at The Mission should decide to build a career there, as Karina had. But in the best families and work environments, there's a certain relational dynamic that plays out over time. It's created when leaders, mentors, or parents invest their time, energy, and training to serve their students, followers, or children out of genuine love and care, and those mentees and children don't just grow up and use the skills they've received; they also carry the same heart to love and serve that was modeled for them. In these environments, beneficiaries are converted into benefactors.

This is the dynamic Jesus established among His apprentices. He said, "Freely you have received; freely give" (Matthew 10:8), and "As I have loved you, so you must love one another" (John 13:34). In the kingdom, the primary evidence that we have received the love of God is that we give it away to others. This is what the Father longs to see in His children—not for His sake, but for theirs.

As a dad myself, I have no desire to force any of my kids to work at my company or take it over when I retire. My investment in their lives is not about securing the future of what I have built but about helping them cultivate a craftsman mindset. Lauren and I loved the journey of helping our kids discover their unique interests and gifts and providing them with support, resources, and opportunities to develop those so they could work in the fields and roles where they would thrive. What matters to us is that they carry a heart to love others, serve, contribute, and form vital and healthy partnerships in those roles. Why? Because we know that this is what will make them happy! It's what makes *us* happy in our own lives.

We've Lost the Love

As we saw in chapter 5, the road to experiencing true passion in our careers and our lives lies not in "following our passion" but in embracing the craftsman mindset that asks, "What do I have to offer the world?" It's not just a mindset of stewardship; it's a mindset of generosity that's focused on helping other people. It's the mindset of Jesus, who knew that the greatest "joy" He could pursue was to lay down His life out of love for us. It's the mindset of every truly great and noble person, who understands that the highest and most rewarding path in life lies in loving and serving others.

Unfortunately, much of our culture today has lost this wisdom that our deepest experiences of joy and passion lie in partnering with, serving, and loving others; and the kind of environments that pass on that wisdom have become more and more rare. The loving, tight-knit community that Jimmy and Genea have created at The Mission, where the orphans experience consistent love and connection and learn to *choose family*, is the unusual exception rather than the rule. Virtually any environment that encourages and facilitates an apprentice or craftsman-like approach to work and life, which involves consistent training and growth in the context of long-term relationships, has rapidly disappeared from today's culture.

Instead, for the last fifty or so years, most people have grown up with experiences of upheaval and rootlessness, largely due to social revolutions (beginning with the Civil Rights movement, Sexual Revolution, Vietnam War, etc.), globalization, and the rise of information technology. Since divorce laws changed in the 1960s, somewhere around half of kids have grown up in broken homes, a deeply destabilizing reality that fractures core family relationships like nothing else. The breakdown of the family, and specifically the high numbers of kids growing up apart from their fathers, has been especially devastating among racial minorities and those with lower income. Postmodern culture has led entire generations to question all forms of authority, walk away from their families and faith communities, and chase new ideologies not based in any rooted traditions or relationships. Nearly every pastor today has to deal with the challenge of high churn and "church hopping" in their congregations. Upward mobility and urbanization have caused many to leave their home communities for training and careers. Education has become increasingly depersonalized and reduced to passing on information rather than modeling and training in personal interactions. Much of corporate culture has embraced and even encouraged a disconnected, transactional style of relationship between employers and employees that breeds little loyalty to a team or organization. Many companies treat their employees like human capital to be used up, and many employees are quick to jump ship when a better offer or opportunity comes along. And our widespread adoption of information technology, which allows us to be constantly "connected" to the flow of information and supposedly to people, actually discourages us from investing time in real, face-to-face relationships with others.

I find it fascinating that the movement encouraging people to "follow your passion" in their careers has arisen in our disconnected culture. Could it be that this movement is telling us to try to find something in our careers that has been lost through the breakdown of relationships and connection, and that's why it's not working out the way we hoped? Could it be that we will find our greatest passion when we find the place, role, and people where we can commit to building long-term partnership and collaboration? Could it be that there is *nothing else* that will actually fix the deepest and most painful problems in our society today?

As I wrote this book, the world was thrown into chaos while dealing with the COVID-19 global pandemic; political, social, and racial upheaval; and a host of related economic, health, and social issues. However, I believe this chaos exposed the deep dysfunction and fracturing of our society due to our underlying crisis of disconnection. It wasn't all negative—battling a new and unknown health threat inspired heroic effort and innovation from men and women working to combat the virus and the economic fallout of global quarantine; many families experienced a season of deeper connection at home; and all the unrest prompted important conversations about justice and the value of all human life. However, the trauma of the pandemic heightened the fear, mistrust, division, and despair that have been growing in our society for many years. The media and internet became war zones of conflicting information and opinions. Incidents of riots, domestic violence, abuse, and suicide spiked across the country. The level of widespread tension, conflict, and division that arose, even in the closest of relationships, was like nothing I've personally seen. The pain and despair caused by disconnection, I would argue, was devastating to people.

These years of upheaval have exposed our desperate need to restore a culture that values humility, listening well, building connection, and serving each other. Thankfully, many people are hungry and seeking ways to do that. More and more people are looking for ways to increase connection in their work lives, from seeking mentorship to starting their own interest groups, teams, collectives, and companies. But if we hope to be successful in this quest for connection, we must be prepared to deal with the issue that lies at the core of all relationships, which every single one of us struggles with on some level, and which is constantly under attack in our culture: *trust.*

The Trust Issue

Our battle with trust is as old as the Bible, which makes it clear that it is a spiritual issue that only God can resolve. In fact, this is arguably the first big truth the Bible presents about the human condition. Genesis 1 and

2 reveal that God's original design for society and culture looked something very much like what the Horners have created at The Mission—a loving family that works together for and with God, collaborating in caring for the world and one another. Genesis 3 gives us the tragic account of how that design began to unravel when Adam and Eve believed the enemy's lies about God and broke trust with Him, which also violated the trust between themselves. Then in Genesis 4, we see how their mistrust passed on to the next generation, with devastating consequences.

Adam, if you remember, was delegated to work the ground and care for the animals. With his two sons, Cain and Abel, division of labor began—Cain became a gardener and Abel tended the flocks. Eventually, the time came for them to show God the results of their labors and receive a performance review. Abel passed his review with flying colors, but God told Cain his work wasn't up to scratch, and Cain became "angry." In psychology, anger is commonly described as a "secondary emotion." When we get angry, it's often a mask for what we're really feeling, which is typically pain, fear, powerlessness, shame, or grief. Unless we uncover these deeper emotions and deal with them in a healthy way, anger will almost always lead us to act out in ways that hurt ourselves and others. God confronted Cain about this and encouraged him to deal with his anger appropriately:

> So the LORD said to Cain, "Why are you angry? And why has your countenance fallen? If you do well, will you not be accepted? And if you do not do well, sin lies at the door. And its desire [is] for you, but you should rule over it." (Genesis 4:6-7, NKJV)

This statement shows that God believed in Cain. God was confident that Cain could do better. He wanted Cain's work to be "accepted." He also believed that Cain had the ability to deal with his emotions and master them so they didn't lead him to do something harmful.

But Cain didn't believe what God believed, and that was the whole problem. Bible scholars and readers have always been curious about why Abel's sacrifice was acceptable to God and Cain's wasn't. Was there something superior about Abel offering an animal sacrifice over Cain bringing an offering of produce from his crops? Was it that Abel gave the "best" of his flock and Cain brought mediocre fruit for his offering? The Bible doesn't give these details, but what it does say is, *"By faith* Abel brought God a better offering than Cain did" (Hebrews 11:4). Translation: Abel deeply trusted and relied on God and knew His heart. Cain did not trust God, and that is revealed in his reaction to God in this moment of failure.

If Cain had trusted God, then even though he had fallen short, he could have looked at God and said, "You're right. It's painful to miss the mark, but I know You still love me. Thank You for showing me where I need to improve and believing that I can do better." He could have looked at Abel and gone, "Wow, bro, well done. You inspire me. I'm going to get to work on my stuff so I can ace my next review like you did." And he could have looked at himself and said, "I failed, but I'm not a failure. I'm going to chalk this up to a learning experience and get back to work."

Instead, in the open wound of his failure, Cain allowed an infection of shame, insecurity, bitterness, and jealousy to grow, which led him to view his relationships with God, his brother, and himself through a lens of mistrust. God was no longer a loving Father but a harsh, unreasonable critic who played favorites. His brother was no longer a coworker whose success was deserved and brought glory to the family but a rival and a threat who had made him look bad. And he was no longer an equally loved and valued son with a bright future ahead but a rejected loser who had disappointed everyone.

Mistrust caused Cain's pain to turn to rage and then to murder, which destroyed all of his relationships—not just with God, his family, and himself, but also with his work. "When you work the ground," God told him, "it will no longer yield its crops for you. You will be a restless wanderer on the earth" (Genesis 4:12). Sure enough, Cain was forced to abandon his career and family and lived as an exile for the rest of his life.

The horror of Abel's murder is not the only thing that makes Cain's story so uncomfortable to read. The problem is that we can all relate to the powerful feelings of anger, shame, insecurity, and jealousy he was wrestling with. At some point, we all get to see others succeeding where we are failing or falling short, and almost all of us will fall into negative comparison. We will also receive painful feedback from someone important in our lives. Though we may not react to these experiences by killing someone, the temptation to react destructively in some way can be strong—in particular, to criticize, push away, or even end our relationships with the people who incited those painful experiences. We may even act destructively to avoid relational pain. Consider Nick's observation that he sees many of his peers leaving jobs and companies to avoid situations where their weaknesses may be exposed and their performance might fall short, because they can't handle the thought of being humiliated in front of their peers or corrected by their boss. They too, like Cain did, are sacrificing their careers because they can't trust others or themselves. The point of Cain's story is that these mistrust-based reactions only bring far more pain into our lives than the original wounds.

The Bible uses this tragic account to invite us to ask what it could look like instead to respond to wounds from a heart of trust rather than mistrust. The whole beauty and challenge in trust is that at its core, trust is about *vulnerability*. Patrick Lencioni says, "In the context of building a team, trust is the confidence among team members that their peers' intentions are good, and that there is no reason to be protective or careful around the group. In essence, *teammates [are] comfortable being vulnerable with one another*."[12] Likewise, Charles Feltman, author of *The Thin Book of Trust: An Essential Primer for Building Trust at Work*, defines trust as "choosing to risk making something you value vulnerable to another person's actions."[13] And vulnerability, by definition, means *exposure to wounding or pain*. There is no such thing as genuine connection, relationship, or partnership without this exposure. Choosing connection means choosing to risk getting hurt. If we hope to build enduring connections, then we must have a plan for dealing with relational wounds from a foundation of trust—not just to avoid the destruction mistrust will cause, but also to preserve the strength and sustenance our family members, friends, colleagues, mentors, and other people bring into our lives.

Lencioni says that trust involves confidence that other people's intentions toward us are good. Psychologists call it the "fundamental attribution error" to give ourselves the benefit of the doubt for having good intentions, which we know we do, while assuming others have bad intentions. We set ourselves up to choose trust when we assume the truth—that other people have the same good intentions we have. In a

---

12 Patrick Lencioni, *The Five Dysfunctions of a Team* (San Francisco, CA: Jossey-Bass, 2002), 195, my emphasis.
13 Charles Feltman, *The Thin Book of Trust: An Essential Primer for Building Trust at Work* (Thin Book Publishing, 2009), Kindle edition, location 77.

painful encounter, it really is true that if we can see that the other person really didn't mean to hurt us, or that if they did, it was intended to be the "wound of a friend" that helped us, it is easier to close the door to bitterness and anger and choose to trust.

If you notice, in Cain's story, none of the pain caused by Abel's success or God's feedback was intended to humiliate or destroy—quite the opposite. The Bible says, "Wounds from a friend can be trusted" (Proverbs 27:6), and "the Lord disciplines the one he loves" (Hebrews 12:6). In loving relationships, we will have wounding experiences that are actually intended to help us see important truths and make changes so we can learn, grow, improve, and excel. I can't tell you how many times my wife, close friends, mentors, and team members have literally *saved* me from making destructive choices because they loved me enough to give me feedback or confront me, show me where I was wrong, and call me higher. We all need this kind of love in our lives, at work, and at home, and the only way to get it is to choose trust.

A Covenant Mindset

Think back and remember the definition of passion we covered in chapter 5—the willingness to endure discomfort and pain for the sake of achieving a great, joyful purpose. And what was the original passion modeled by Jesus? Jesus' great, joyful purpose was restoring the broken connection between us and the Father—and by extension, our broken connection with each other and ourselves. He was passionate about dealing with the root of our trust issues and showing us, once and for all, that God loved us and had nothing but good intentions for us. Jesus laid His life down to restore our ability to experience family and partnership as the Father originally designed.

This is why Jesus is "the mediator of a new covenant" whose "sprinkled blood . . . speaks a better word than the blood of Abel" (Hebrews 12:24). "Covenant" is the biblical term for Genea and Jimmy's definition of family—it is relationship that you choose and commit to for the long term out of love. The blood of Abel spoke the word of broken covenant. It was because the ground had received Abel's blood, the evidence of Cain's violation of their relationship, that it could no longer partner with Cain and yield its fruit to him. But Jesus' blood speaks the word of restored covenant. Because of His sacrifice, we now have a spiritual resource that enables us to overcome the pitfalls of mistrust and build the kind of relationships that can endure the wounds that will inevitably come—and be stronger for it. That resource, quite simply, is the love of the Father. This love "always trusts" (1 Corinthians 13:7).

One of the themes in the story of Cain and Abel is that our trust issues with others and ourselves are ultimately rooted in our trust issues with God. We see the same theme in the parable of the talents: the fearful worker didn't put himself out there and take risks to invest and grow what the business owner had given him because he didn't trust him. Scripture is full of examples of people—and in the Old Testament, the entire nation of Israel—making tragic choices that had painful consequences for themselves and others because in their core, they didn't trust God, didn't wait for Him, didn't listen to Him, and didn't press into Him when things were difficult. But Jesus' entire mission was, through demonstrating His great love for us on the cross and giving us His Spirit to connect directly with Him, to heal and save us from this inability to trust God. He came to restore our ability to walk in covenant relationship with Him, ourselves, and others.

I realize that "covenant" is probably not a word most of us think of in relation to our work lives and partnerships. But my goal in this chapter is to argue that the passion we are seeking in what we *do* cannot be found apart from *who* we are doing it with and for, and specifically, apart from the relational context of deep trust and connection with God and others. And covenant is that relational context. To be clear, not all covenant relationships look alike. Marriage is a lifelong commitment to love one person, while work partnerships are likely to change as our projects and assignments change. But covenant is also a mindset and approach to all types of relationships that say, "I am committed to the health and strength of this connection. I'm not here just to get something from you, but for us to both contribute so we can enrich each other's life. I'm not going to bail on you when things get tough. I'm going to lean into the discomfort, tell the truth, let you tell me the truth, and believe the best about both of us. I'm going to hold on to trust."

The covenant mindset is a long-term mindset. It recognizes that the richest benefits of relationship only come through trust, and that it often takes years of investment in a relationship for deep, enduring trust to be established. Grand gestures in the moment don't build trust; consistent small gestures over time do. Specifically, as I explain in *The Business of Honor*, the gestures that build trust in any relationship fall into three main buckets: telling the truth, receiving well, and serving well. When we approach people and relationships with a covenant mindset, we focus first on practicing these things, and then on looking for others to reciprocate. Ultimately, we want to make our greatest investment in the relationships where there is reciprocity and mutual commitment.

Here's how that has played out in my consulting practice, for example. I should start by saying that I only started using the term "consulting" after I began writing and speaking, to create an on-ramp for engaging with people who reach out to me through those venues and want one-on-one time with me. I approach them as I have approached everyone I have met with over the years. Basically, I just "hang out" with people and have a conversation with them. I really don't want them to see me as a "mentor," "coach," or "consultant." I want them to see me as someone who is interested in building a connection with them, a connection in which I plan to listen, receive, and be impacted as much as I intend to speak, give, and influence.

Every time, these conversations progress from the external to the internal. The person will tell me about what they're working on and the current challenges they're facing with their project, team, business, or organization. I ask lots of questions so that I understand not only what they're dealing with but also their perspective and attitude toward it. Usually before long, I have enough information to start filling in details of the story they haven't given me, because I have seen and experienced them countless times myself and can now easily discern them. I often share openly about how I made mistakes and learned lessons in similar situations, and I offer some strategies and tactics for how they can fix problems and be more successful. But then I start to lean in and challenge them about what I'm seeing in their heart and mind—problematic beliefs, insecurities, or ambitions that are holding them back from genuine growth.

For example, I recently met with a man in his mid-twenties who had been put in charge of a sales team and was struggling with a cluster of leadership issues. As we pressed deeper into the dynamics he was trying to navigate, he finally admitted that he just wanted to know how to control these people and get them to do what he needed them to do. I smiled, because I felt his pain, which is the pain of every leader and parent from the beginning of time.

"It's frustrating, isn't it?" I said. "But as my friend Danny Silk always says, you can't control other people. The only person you can control—on a good day—is yourself. If you learn that now and start focusing on what you are going to do, how you're going to live out what's important to you, then you'll lead by example. And you'll set the tone for what's expected on your team."

This turned us on to the topic of what was most important to this young man, and together we uncovered what was perhaps his deepest need and motivation at this stage of his life: he wanted significance—to be significant and to do significant things. So I asked him, "How do you define significance?"

He thought for a moment and said, "To win souls for Christ."

It was obvious to me that this was what he thought to be the "right" answer but was not the real answer, so I called him on it. "Nope. That's not what's burning in you. What if I told you that you are already significant, and what you are doing right now is significant? What if significance for you is to become a great leader and kill it as a salesman? What if it's taking all the wisdom you're gaining in leading people into a marriage and learning how to serve and lead your wife and kids? What if it's putting on display what a life of partnership with God looks like?"

It seemed to be a new thought for him—and a liberating one. I could actually see the shift that was beginning to happen in him as he saw his purpose, assignment, and passion through fresh eyes.

But as much as I was energized by helping him toward an aha

moment, I also knew that this was just the first of what could be many conversations over years. Because that is what I sign up for when someone gives me the honor of speaking into their lives at a heart level. I'm signing up for a relational journey, and relational journeys don't usually conform to short or artificial timelines. Some of the people I "hang out" with take what they get from our conversations and just get to work on their stuff right away, with impressive results. Others seem to struggle or just operate with a different urgency and timeline. For one person I met with on multiple occasions, it took five years before they began to implement some of the action steps I'd repeatedly urged them to take. And then there are a few people who get mad and frustrated and walk away. Those are the ones who break your heart.

Do I enjoy working with action-oriented people more? Sure. Do I need to exercise discernment and boundaries with people who want my time and advice but don't seem interested in taking it to heart? Absolutely. But as a covenant-minded person, I don't write anyone off. The people I naturally like are fun to walk with, but it's the tough cases that not only help me practice and strengthen my relational skills, but they also help me grow in understanding the Father's heart for all people. The Father doesn't write off any of His children.

The Only Powerful Choice

At my stage of life, I am blessed to have a marriage, friendships, and partnerships that span decades, and I can tell you that signing up for these long relational journeys has shaped me more profoundly than anything else in my life. Sticking it out, year after year, through all the seasons and challenges that life can throw at us, is what gives us the opportunity to build the kind of relational skills and wisdom we need to build and protect connection.

I think many people today are hesitant to sign up for the long journey because they're afraid of being hurt and won't know what to do if they get hurt. But a covenant mindset recognizes that the longer the journey and closer the connection, the more inevitable it becomes that we will experience pain and wounding in our areas of vulnerability. Our weaknesses, fears, and core beliefs about each other will come to the surface. Any area of fear, shame, or mistrust in our hearts will be exposed, and that exposure will be uncomfortable. And the only way to respond to this is to do what it takes to confront the pain, deal with it, and strengthen the relationship on the other side of it. These moments of exposure are the moments in which we make the most important choices of our lives, the choices by which we decide who we are going to be. Will we allow the pain of fear, shame, and mistrust to drive us, as they drove Adam, Eve, and Cain, onto the destructive path of self-protection, blame-shifting, hiding, and destroying relationships? Or will we recognize the opportunity to go to God, deal with these issues in our hearts, and choose to work it out with people?

My friend Danny Silk writes and speaks extensively about this topic of how choosing connection, again and again, is the most powerful and important choice we make in life. It's how we become *powerful people*:

> A healthy, lasting relationship can only be built between two people who choose one another and take full responsibility for that choice. This choice must be based on who they are, what they want, and what they are committed to doing as individuals . . . In order to be able

to make and keep commitments like this— commitments to enduring, intimate relationships—you need to be a certain kind of person. You need to be a powerful person. Powerful people take responsibility for their lives and choices. Powerful people choose who they want to be with, what they are going to pursue in life, and how they are going to go after it.[14]

When I consider the people in my life who I would call "powerful," they all match this description. They aren't domineering or needing to be the center of attention. They are people of passion, vision, discipline, hard work, and joy—all of which flow out of their deep love for God, themselves, and others.

If we want to be wise apprentices who can receive the wisdom from teachers and mentors we need to excel in our craft, wise workers who can benefit and serve others well, and wise leaders who build partnerships, teams, and organizations that create impact in the world, then our choice is clear. If we want to experience the passion and joy of healthy relationships at work, at home, and in life, then our choice is clear. We must reject the path of fear and mistrust, lean into God and others, and choose to do the work of connection.

14 Danny Silk, *Keep Your Love On: Connection Communication and Boundaries* (Redding, CA: Printopya, 2015), Kindle edition, 20.

"The challenge of work life balance is without a question one of the most significant struggles faced by modern man."

Steven Covey, author

CHAPTER 8

What Is Work-Life Balance, Anyway?

When I talk with people about their work lives, one topic that typically arises is work-life balance. While most agree that work-life balance is important, I've found that people differ about what it means and looks like.

Some people are idealists. For them, work-life balance is all about crafting each day so that it includes everything they want to do or feel they should be doing—morning devotions, exercise, meal planning, work, time with friends or family, etc. Others describe an ideal work week that usually involves fewer than forty hours of work, leaving plenty of time for "self-care," hobbies, and other activities. Still others talk about an ideal life where they "have it all"—good health, a successful job, a happy family, great friends, a nice home and car, fun vacations, and some kind of meaningful contribution to the world.

Then there are the survivalists—people who are somewhere between overwhelmed, overworked, and burned out. These people talk about work-life balance in terms of a struggle, an impossible goal, or a luxury they can't really afford. They either want to find ways to escape from work or feel hopeless to overcome the cycles of stress in which they feel trapped.

The more I've observed the idealists and survivalists, the more I've become convinced that they are missing the same thing: a clear and compelling vision for their life, built on their identity, purpose, and assignment, that enables them to connect what they're doing in the present with what they want to achieve in the long term. This leaves the idealists endlessly looking for tools, shortcuts, or "hacks" to achieve the perfect day or week, or a snapshot of the perfect life, and the survivalists looking for moments to relieve enough pressure to get them through another day. In the end, neither really achieves any real, sustainable balance.

People with a vision of their identity, purpose, and assignment, on the other hand, have a very different approach to work-life balance—something that was confirmed for me when I interviewed Nick, Katrina, and Victor for this book. In our conversations, none of them talked about either trying to fulfill some ideal checklist or survive their life. Instead, their descriptions of work-life balance centered around three basic disciplines that flow from their vision-driven approach to their lives:

1. Clarify your current assignment.
2. Give everything to your current assignment.
3. Say no to everything that is not part of your current assignment.

I believe these disciplines form the core of building a wise approach to work-life balance. Let's take a closer look at each one.

Clarify Your Current Assignment

As I said in chapter 6, your current assignment is more than just your current job. It is the complete picture of the roles, relationships, and resources for which you are presently responsible. Clarifying your current assignment means finding a way to put this picture in front of you, seeking to understand it through the framework of your identity and purpose (which is where you get your core values and long-term objectives in life), and then organizing it according to priority.

When we start looking for this picture of our current assignment, I think we quickly discover that the very concept of work-life balance starts to break down a bit. The term "work-life balance" suggests that we can compartmentalize our lives into two main buckets: work (paid employment) and non-work (relationships, hobbies, rest, etc.). But these compartments aren't actually helpful when it comes to trying to organize our lives or find balance. For one, many of the non-work activities we are responsible for actually involve significant amounts of work. For another, most of us aren't trying to balance two areas of our lives—we're trying to balance at least four or five. This compartmentalized approach is not going to help us paint an accurate picture of our current assignment.

When we look to Scripture, I don't think we find any examples of breaking our lives up into work or non-work activities except for the obvious one: "Remember the Sabbath day by keeping it holy. Six days you shall labor and do all your work, but the seventh day is a sabbath to the LORD your God" (Exodus 20:8-10). The idea behind the Sabbath is that God designed our lives to have a weekly rhythm of work and rest. Trying to operate without this rhythm is one of the quickest and most obvious ways we get out of balance. It's not a coincidence to me that our widespread concern with work-life balance has arisen since we've gotten rid of the tradition of having most businesses and activities close down on Sundays. I'm not saying we have to go back to that, but I do think it supported a cultural rhythm of rest that was healthier than the 24/7 work life we now embrace. If our lives are feeling out of balance, looking at our work-rest rhythm is the first thing we should check on. If you can't remember the last time you took a full day to rest from work, unplug from your devices, worship God, and celebrate the good things in your life, then your life is probably off balance, and finding that rhythm will help you reclaim balance.

However, in the biblical view, rest and work don't belong in separate buckets. They are related and integral parts of living a full life, just as recovery is related to exercise, and both are part of being fit and healthy. The Bible always encourages us to approach our lives holistically. For example, one of the most interesting pictures of work-life balance in the Bible is one you've probably never thought of as a picture of work-life balance. Proverbs 31 is usually taught as the picture of the "ideal woman." However, Bible scholars argue that this poem is a description of personified Wisdom praised throughout the book of Proverbs. And Wisdom looks like a person who is living their whole life in a certain way:

> A wife of noble character who can find? She is worth far more than rubies.
> Her husband has full confidence in her and lacks nothing of value.
> She brings him good, not harm, all the days of her life.
> She selects wool and flax and works with eager hands.
> She is like the merchant ships, bringing her food from afar.

She gets up while it is still night; she provides food for her family and portions for her female servants.

She considers a field and buys it; out of her earnings she plants a vineyard.

She sets about her work vigorously; her arms are strong for her tasks.

She sees that her trading is profitable, and her lamp does not go out at night.

In her hand she holds the distaff and grasps the spindle with her fingers.

She opens her arms to the poor and extends her hands to the needy.

When it snows, she has no fear for her household; for all of them are clothed in scarlet.

She makes coverings for her bed; she is clothed in fine linen and purple.

Her husband is respected at the city gate, where he takes his seat among the elders of the land.

She makes linen garments and sells them, and supplies the merchants with sashes. She is clothed with strength and dignity; she can laugh at the days to come.

She speaks with wisdom, and faithful instruction is on her tongue.

She watches over the affairs of her household and does not eat the bread of idleness. Her children arise and call her blessed; her husband also, and he praises her:

"Many women do noble things, but you surpass them all."
(Proverbs 31:10-29, NIV)

If we try to put this picture of a wise, balanced life into work and non-work buckets, it doesn't really make sense. One could argue that this wise woman is *always* working. Her life is a picture of multiple roles—wife, mother, employer, craftswoman, household manager, and community benefactor—and her responsibilities in these roles are all woven together, not divided into compartments. The expression of her wisdom is that she is fulfilling her responsibilities in a way that produces good results for her marriage, children, employees, home, business, and community—and her own emotional health. She is clearly not burned out or in survival mode but is energized by joy and love as she works strategically to meet the present, immediate needs of the day (feeding her family and employees) and to build for the future (saving money, buying land, planting a vineyard, making goods to sell, preparing her home for the winter, etc.).

Proverbs 31 is an amazing picture of what a wise worker with a balanced, thriving, fruitful life looks like. Of course, it's important that we don't look at this picture and go into shame and condemnation when we compare it to where we are now. This chapter is in the Bible to show us what is available to us if we stay on our journey of apprenticeship with the Lord and steward our assignments well.

One metaphor that fits well with building a holistic picture of our current assignment is to think of our lives as a garden with various types of plants or crops that represent multiple departments of our lives. My wife, Lauren, is a brilliant gardener who has turned our home and property into a paradise of flowers, roses, citrus trees, shrubs, and raised vegetable beds. I have loved watching her passion to invest time, energy, and resources into planning each area of her garden, learning exactly what each plant needs to thrive, and then doing the year-round, seasonal, and even daily cultivation necessary to bring growth and flourishing. Cultivating our lives, like cultivating a garden, is an art and a science that requires us to learn how to work in each area of our lives, which include:

- Relationships (God, spouse, kids, friends, work colleagues, etc.)
- Personal health (physical, psychological, spiritual)
- Employment (what you do to make a living)
- Other meaningful activities (hobbies, causes, groups)
- Maintenance (chores, bills, etc.)

Each of these crops needs certain things, not just to survive, but to thrive and be fruitful. Clarifying our assignment is all about getting a vision for thriving and fruitfulness in each of these areas and identifying their current needs so we can give them the attention and nurture they deserve.

One exercise to help you do this is to make a list of your primary roles and responsibilities in each of these five areas or "plots" of your garden. For example:

RELATIONSHIPS	
Roles	God: Son/Daughter Marriage: Husband/Wife Family: Parent Friendships: Friend Work: Colleague, Boss, Employee, etc. Community: Contributor, Volunteer, etc.
Responsibilities	Trusting, obeying Partnering, loving, supporting Protecting, providing, leading, nurturing Encouraging, connecting Collaborating, teamwork Serving

`PERSONAL HEALTH	
Roles	Being God's temple
Responsibilities	Caring for body, soul, and spirit

EMPLOYMENT	
Roles	Worker (specify)
Responsibilities	Performing tasks, fulfilling goals, etc. (specify)

MEANINGFUL ACTIVITIES	
Roles	Hobbyist, Group Member, Cause Supporter (specify)
Responsibilities	Developing skills and interests and contributing for recreation and service

MAINTENANCE	
Roles	Manager
Responsibilities	Maintaining home, property, resources

Once you have created this list, consider each "plot" one by one (you can also get as granular as you want and break them down into subplots) and ask three questions:

1. What does it look like for this plot in my garden to be thriving?
2. What is the primary thing I need to be cultivating in this area of my life in this current season?
3. What are 1 to 3 things I should be doing consistently to cultivate that thing?

An exercise like this does require time and reflection, but the clarity it brings to our current assignment is incredibly beneficial. It doesn't have to be full of anxiety, either. Remember, the One who gives us our assignments is not a scary taskmaster, like the lazy worker in the parable of the talents imagined his boss to be. He is our loving Father. He has entrusted these things to us so that we can discover and develop the potential He put in us, and step into the privilege and joy of being His apprentices and partners. He doesn't want us to see our assignments as a heavy burden but as a joyful opportunity to thrive and be fruitful, to experience *abundant life*. So as you clarify your vision of both your long-term purpose and your current assignment, lean in to hear His voice and gain His perspective.

One of the things I loved hearing Katrina talk about was how her vision for her current assignment took shape through dreaming with God and pursuing prophetic words she's received through her life. She told me about one word in particular she received in her early twenties from a woman who said, "I can see you growing gray on a farm. God really wants you to keep listening because He's going to give you strategy every decade. So keep your ear to the ground."

"That word planted the idea that I just needed to stay in tune with God's voice because He was going to keep giving me new ideas," Katrina told me. "It also encouraged me to start getting a vision for things I hadn't seen before. When you're twenty-two years old and you barely have enough money to buy shampoo, the idea of trying to come up with $1 million to buy a farm is just hard to see. I didn't even have $1,000. But the prophetic word invited me to start imagining my future ten, twenty, thirty, and forty years down the road."

This discipline of staying present to what the Lord is saying in the moment, while asking Him to help us form strategic vision for the years to come, is probably our most powerful key to staying clear on our assignments. It is also what enables us to look to our present and our future with joy, which energizes us to get up every day and give everything we have to our current assignment.

Give Everything to Your Current Assignment

When I asked Nick about his approach to work-life balance, he began by explaining where he fundamentally differed from many of his peers in his overall vision of what balance was all about.

"In our culture of social media and instant gratification, work-life balance has come to mean achieving a certain lifestyle for many in my generation," he said. "We look at Instagram and see people on vacation in Bali, so we want to go to Bali. Never mind that we only have $400 in our bank accounts and can't pay our rent. So, we live above and beyond our means and ask for as much personal time off as we can get so we can convince everyone we're living some kind of lavish lifestyle."

For Nick, the idea of working to achieve a lifestyle of wealth and leisure isn't inspiring. The people he looks up to—the people he thinks model a life well-lived—are not those taking exotic vacations, driving expensive cars, or showing off their private boats and planes. Rather, he is drawn to people who are "the best at what they do, make history, and have massive impact." For these people, what matters is working to achieve specific long-term goals over their lifetime, and balance is defined by what it takes to achieve those goals.

"One of my favorite Bible verses is Genesis 49:27," Nick said. "'Benjamin is a ravenous wolf; in the morning he devours the prey, in the evening he divides the plunder.' I think this verse is actually talking about work-life balance over the span of your whole life. In the morning, when you're young, it's your job to go out and devour your prey. Fulfill your purpose and accumulate what you need to accumulate. And then when you're older, if you've worked hard enough, you will have spoils to divide. If you don't work hard enough, you will never have spoils to divide. You have to go out and attack your assignments every day."

Katrina shares this commitment to attacking her assignments—not because she's hustling to survive and stay afloat, but out of a deep sense of love and honor for God and the people she serves, and also because it's *fun*.

"I have had this recurring dream about a puppy dog who is desperately eager to play ball with its owner," she told me. "I've realized it's a picture of how God wants us to dream with Him. He is constantly throwing balls at us in the form of our passions and work, and it's our pleasure to go run after that ball and bring it back to Him. God just keeps throwing ideas at me about what I could add to the farm, and then I find it really easy to run after that ball. I just have a green light to go after it until I hit a wall."

Katrina also explained that it has been in this context of giving everything she has to her assignments that she has learned her most important lessons about balance. A few years into developing multiple sub-businesses on her farm, she began to recognize areas where she needed to adjust so that she could grow the business successfully and not burn out.

"When you start a business, you just throw everything you have at it," she explained. "So I definitely didn't have balance at first. For the first few years, every day I got up really early, worked nonstop, sometimes wouldn't eat till dinner, and went to bed late. The work kept growing because I kept adding projects. Initially, these projects coincided with the normal rhythm of the farm. For example, we added the wedding venue to do events during the summer and the harvest season, which meant we still had a slower season in the winter. But then we built our tasting room/restaurant, which is open year-round, and started doing more brewing and fermentation during the winter months. So, at some point the Holy Spirit and my friends began to nudge me to make sure I was taking care of myself. They helped me see that there was never going to be any time in my day to feed myself and exercise unless I made time for it. It also became clear to me that the only way I was going to be able to run this expanded business successfully into my fifties and sixties was if I started taking better care of my body. So I committed to lifting weights five mornings a week and meal planning. It was a bit of an adjustment—I had to get my main foreman and crew set up to start the day without me and understand that this was going to be the new game plan. But nobody had a meltdown. I got healthier and so did my businesses."

There's something so appropriate about Katrina choosing to lift weights to achieve more balance in her life. The first definition of the word "balance" in the Oxford American Dictionary is "an even distribution of weight enabling someone or something to remain upright and steady." Your current assignment encompasses the full weight of responsibility that rests on your shoulders at this moment in time. The only way you're going to achieve balance is by letting that full weight rest on you and fully engaging all your energies and skill to carry it well. As you do this consistently, your strength, skill, and capacity will expand, enabling you to take on even greater levels of responsibility. That is the goal of a successful apprenticeship: to grow in our skills and abilities to handle more complex tasks and workload so we can achieve mastery.

Say No to Everything That Is Not Part of Your Current Assignment

To continue the weightlifting metaphor, one of the most common ways we get out of balance is by taking on weight God has not asked us to carry. Along with failing to practice a healthy rhythm of work and rest, these distractions, which often take the form of extra responsibilities, are the greatest source of imbalance in our lives.

One of the main reasons it is so critical to clarify our assignments and then give ourselves fully to them is that this is the best way to discern what we need to be saying no to. When I asked Victor how he practices work-life balance, he said that one of the guiding principles he has operated by throughout his life is that "Whatever you say yes to means you're saying no to something else." We can't protect our yes to our current assignment unless we are willing and prepared to say no to things that would threaten or compromise our ability to follow through on that commitment. As Danny Silk explains in *Keep Your Love On*, successfully building a life and relationships that are healthy and thriving requires us to set and honor healthy boundaries around the things that are import-ant to us. This looks like telling ourselves and others what we're going to do and what we're not going to do, and following through with both.

Many of the things we need to say no to will become clear when we do vision-building exercises like the one I described earlier in this chap-ter. Laying out the "plots" of our garden with their roles, responsibilities, and goals gives us a framework for recognizing where our limits need to be so we can focus on what we're cultivating in our current season. But as we move toward this vision, we will have to keep working to define our yeses and our nos as we discover what it actually takes to follow through with our yes.

When Katrina said yes to adding more businesses on her farm, for example, she didn't yet know what that would require of her and the limits she would need to set. Eventually she reached a point where she saw that she was spreading herself too thin with everything she had on her plate. Along with making space for health and exercise, she stepped down from a number of nonprofit boards in the community where she had been volunteering.

"I got a lot of pushback when I stepped down from the boards," she admitted. "I'm a go-getter and they really wanted me there to help fundraise. But it was threatening my ability to focus on what I was doing on the farm. Once I cut the fat of my yeses, especially the ones I felt guilted into, I got laser-focused back on my business and had this fresh love and energy to give it. Maybe when I'm old and gray I can do more volunteering."

I told Katrina that that was exactly what I did. For nearly forty years, I kept my head down building my business. I went to church and home group and supported my children in their various activities, but I wasn't volunteering on mission trips or getting involved in various church and school projects like Lauren was. I wasn't traveling, consulting, writing, or speaking. There were a lot of things I said no to for a long time that I now can say yes to because my company and kids are mature and I'm in a new season.

Contrary to what many people seem to think, embracing the limits of our current assignment is incredibly freeing. It's a tragic mistake to hold off on saying yes to what God has put in front of us because we're afraid of commitment and afraid of missing out. The only way we will actually miss out on the opportunity to build a thriving, fruitful, balanced life is by holding back from a fully engaged yes to our current assignment. Yes, it can be hard to say no to seemingly good things, like helping nonprofits. You might have to work through some feelings of frustration or jealousy when you see other people doing or having things you'd like to do or have right now. But all of these things ultimately bring us back to the core issue at the foundation of building a healthy, thriving, balanced life, and that is trusting God. We must trust that He knows us, loves us, wants to bless us, and has tailor-made our current assignment to help us grow as His apprentice toward mastery in life.

Mess Is Part of Mastery

One reason I like to think of cultivating a balanced life as tending a garden is that in gardening, there's a lot of dirt involved. It's messy. So is life. But the dirt is where things grow from. God knows this. He even set it up this way. He is not afraid of struggle, mistakes, or failures. In fact, He knows that it's when things don't work out, when things get out of balance, that we have our greatest opportunities to learn wisdom about how He designed us to work and live.

One of things I love about Nick is that he's not afraid to fail. In fact, he knows he will meet failure, setbacks, and all kinds of challenges as he pursues his purpose and assignment. This doesn't mean that he is plunging recklessly ahead without a plan for success. He told me he spent an entire year working on the plan for his company, and one of the main things he did in this process was try to figure out everything that could possibly go wrong with his plan. When he finally launched the company, he knew that he would still encounter problems he hadn't foreseen, but the exercise of preparing for failure had honed and strengthened his commitment to push through them and learn from them rather than give up.

"Too many people start a business without a clear purpose and plan, and then when things go bad, they stop," Nick told me. "Your plan will not happen the way that you envision it, but if you're clear on your purpose, you will pivot and be persistent rather than throwing in the towel. Success never happens on a linear path. It takes a Z route."

Sure enough, Nick encountered a major setback within the first few years of starting his company. He hired a CFO who made some bad financial decisions and then left the company, leaving Nick in the worst financial position of his life.

"For a while, I didn't know how I was going to pay rent," he said. "If I hadn't had faith in what I was doing, I probably wouldn't have made it through that moment. But even when I couldn't see how, I kept praying and I knew I would come through. I kept waking up and doing what I needed to do, even when it was hard. And eventually, the doors started opening."

"When things go incredibly wrong or incredibly right, both are unbelievable in the moment," he continued. "You're not going to get an understanding in that moment. But now that a couple of years have passed since that difficult season, I can see that I would not be where I am right now if I hadn't had those struggles."

There is no season or assignment of our lives where we will not have to endure some kind of pain or sacrifice as we cultivate our gardens. But the more we strengthen our ability to live from a vision for both our long-term purpose and our short-term assignments, the more we will lean into this pain and leverage it for our growth. More and more, we will see every failure and challenge as an essential and valuable part of our journey toward mastery in life.

Remember, as Genesis 1 and 2 show us, it was always God's plan for us to partner with Him in taking an undeveloped planet and causing it to flourish. This is what it means to "rule, subdue, and take dominion." We were designed to take things in chaos and bring them into order, to see problems and create solutions, to take things that are out of balance and bring them into balance. This is what the Bible calls "reigning in life" (Romans 5:17). Reigning in life is not about getting out of survival mode and achieving some perfect picture of a "balanced" life that has no more problems to solve. It is recognizing that in every season and assignment of life, we are engaged in a dynamic process of bringing specific things into order and helping them function so they can flourish. And it's through that process that we grow and become who we were created to be.

"The shorter way to do many things is
to only do one thing at a time."

Mozart

CHAPTER 9

Becoming a Wise Resource Manager

I once consulted with a newlywed couple, Mark and Faith, whose long-term goal was to buy a house and start a family. They had recently inherited some money, which would nearly cover the down payment on the house they wanted. However, they weren't sure if they could afford the monthly mortgage payments, higher utilities, and all the other expenses that would come with owning this home.

I asked them some questions to learn more about their financial situation, and soon learned that they had never prepared a budget. So, I asked them to come to our next meeting with recent bank statements and a report showing their take-home income (what they actually deposited in the bank on a weekly, semi-weekly, or monthly basis) and living expenses (rent, insurance, gas, groceries, phone bill, etc.) so we could go through it together.

When Mark and Faith showed me their financial documents, I quickly noticed that the disposable income (what was left after covering their living expenses) listed in their report seemed high compared to what they actually had in their bank account. Their spending on groceries, however, seemed low. After doing a quick mental calculation I asked, "So, can you tell me how you both live on six dollars of food per day?"

"Where do you get that number?" Mark asked.

"I divided what you spend on groceries each month by thirty days in a month. But I'm guessing that's not right. Does someone give you food money or meals?"

Mark and Faith explained that as they were in ministry, it was fairly common for people to invite them out to a meal and pay for it, but this happened at most once or twice a week. So I said, "Take me through a normal day. When you wake up, what do you eat?"

"Well, on our way to work, we usually stop for lattes," Faith said. "I'll get a pastry and Mark usually gets a breakfast sandwich."

This twenty-dollar purchase, repeated every day for twenty work days a month, meant they were spending around four hundred dollars a month on breakfast. We then discovered that an additional two hundred dollars was going out each month to cover coffee or meals when Faith and Mark took various people out for "mentor meetings." They were also eating out with friends after home group each week, going for date nights twice a month, paying for a number of phone apps and a gym membership they weren't using, and spending over a hundred dollars a month on gifts for friends and special occasions.

"This is great!" I told them enthusiastically, after we finished our investigation. "Now we know where your money is going. We also know you need to come up with about $X per month to cover the mortgage and bills on your dream home. So let's talk about what you could do to manage your finances toward meeting that goal."

I began to lay out a list of suggestions for them. Cutting the useless apps and gym membership seemed like a no-brainer. The rest of the suggestions involved some creativity. For starters, they could free up around three hundred dollars a month if they started having coffee and breakfast at home in the mornings. Doing their "mentor meetings" at home, in a park, at an office, or during a walk could save further money on meals. They could also spend less on home group and date nights by sharing meals, eating at home and then just going out for dessert, or bringing food if appropriate. Finally, I suggested that instead of buying gifts at the store, they could explore the many options for low-cost, homemade gifts available on the internet these days.

If they took all of these suggestions, I explained, they could potentially free up close to *80 percent* of what they needed to pay for their new home each month. Even if they modified the suggestions somewhat—for example, reducing five coffee breakfasts a week down to two—they could access a significant amount of cash they already had and point it toward their big goal.

As I had anticipated, Faith and Mark liked some of my suggestions more than others. Faith was excited by the idea of making more gifts, as she loved to bake and create art pieces. But the thing both of them found most challenging to think about was giving up their morning Starbucks ritual. When I asked them why this was the case, they explained that this was the common practice among their friends, most of whom weren't in ministry. They felt that they were working just as hard as their friends and deserved to be able to enjoy at least some aspects of the same lifestyle.

"That may be true," I responded. "The point of this exercise is not to tell you what you deserve or don't deserve, or even what to do or not to do. The point is to get clarity on where your money is currently going and ask yourselves, 'What do we really want?' You might decide that maintaining your current lifestyle is more important than moving toward the goal of buying a house. Or you may decide that you're going to stop hiding the money you need for your house in the cash register at Starbucks every week. It's entirely up to you."

Mark and Faith thanked me for my help and advice, but I sensed their discomfort and disappointment as they left that meeting. I think part of them was hoping I would just pray for the money they needed to show up miraculously, instead of requiring them to do this deep dive into how they were managing their money. I wasn't too surprised, therefore, when I didn't hear from Mark and Faith for a few months. When I did, however, I was pleasantly surprised to hear them tell me they had made some significant changes to their lifestyle and were making real progress toward being able to afford their dream home.

"I was pretty frustrated when we left that meeting with you," Mark confessed with a chuckle. "I really did not want to give up those lattes. But every time I walked into the coffee shop, I couldn't help thinking about the house. Finally, I just had to stop because I didn't like feeling that I was saying no to the house every time I got coffee."

"Congratulations!" I responded happily. "This is what mastering your money is all about—using it to achieve the things that really matter to you in the long term."

I continued to encourage Mark and Faith and consult with them on strategies for how to increase their income and manage their expenses. Within a year of our first meeting, Mark and Faith had closed escrow on their new home.

Stewardship and the Art of Limits

I meet many people like Faith and Mark—good-hearted people who love Jesus, love people, and want to do good in the world. Many of them are working faithfully at their jobs and attempting to live within their means by not going into massive debt or making big purchases they can't afford. (I also meet some who are not working hard or trying to live within their means at all—but that's another conversation.) But when it comes to dreaming of their future and working toward their goals, they have leveled off. They can't see how to get from where they are to where they want to be without some kind of divine intervention. All of their resources are tied up in maintaining their current lifestyle and none seem to be available to help them grow a legacy. And many of them think that this is what "stewardship" looks like—using resources to stay afloat in life and enjoy a few creature comforts along the way.

But Scripture is clear that stewardship is about using resources in a way that causes them to grow. We see this in the parable of the talents—the wise workers put their boss's money to work and doubled it. We also see it more fully in the picture of the Proverbs 31 woman we looked at in the last chapter. In fact, this poem beautifully depicts what it looks like to manage not only money but all three primary resources we have in life—time, energy, and money (or material possessions)—as wise workers. Let's briefly take a look at how the wise woman stewards these three things.

When it comes to how she uses her time, we see that the wise woman is neither busy and running around as many of us are, bound by the tyranny of the urgent, nor is she lying around drinking mimosas and bingeing shows on Netflix. She "gets up while it is still night" and "her lamp does not go out at night" (vv. 15, 18). She "watches over the affairs of her household and does not eat the bread of idleness" (v. 27). Yet she also "can laugh at the days to come" because she isn't stressing about being behind on things or not feeling prepared for what lies ahead (v. 25).

When it comes to energy, the wise woman "works with eager hands" and "sets about her work vigorously; her arms are strong for her tasks" (vv. 13, 17). In Hebrew, that word "eager" means "pleasure" and "delight." Whether it's making fine garments, investing in land, planting crops, selling her wares, or preparing food for her children, employees, and the needy, this wise woman does it all with skill and power born of genuine and passionate love for what she is doing. The word "strong" means not only physical strength but also mental and emotional strength—*courage*. This woman is *all in* with what she is doing, taking risks to develop and use her skills. She's not playing it safe with her energy; she is fully engaged in her tasks and assignments.

And when it comes to her money and material resources, the wise woman seems to have three priorities. First, she uses them to produce things of *excellence*. She makes, wears, and sells garments and coverings of the best quality (see vv. 21-22). Second, she uses them to produce things that *benefit* other people. And third, she uses them to *reproduce* more material resources so she can sustain her ability to produce excellent things that help people.

This poem shows us that wise workers use their resources with high levels of passion and purpose. On the one hand, there is incredible focus and economy in this model of stewardship. We get the sense that nothing under this wise woman's management is being wasted or neglected. Everything is being used to its maximum potential. At the same time, she also lives with great abundance, generosity, and margin. We get the sense that every need she is responsible to meet in her family, business, and community will be met and then some.

There's actually a word that captures both of these dimensions of wise stewardship: "thrift." While most of us associate thrift with being a penny pincher or a store where you can buy secondhand goods, the word originally comes from the word "thrive." It meant *prosperity*—prosperity that can only come about through the wise use of resources. Wise stewardship is using our resources so that every area of our lives becomes fruitful and thriving.

In the last chapter, we saw that work-life balance, as displayed in Proverbs 31, is about managing the plots of our garden in a way that meets present-day needs while also planning for the future. Similarly, wise stewardship of our resources only comes into focus when we build a vision that connects our short-term assignments with our long-term purpose and passion. This was the beauty of what happened with Mark and Faith. They saw that they were pointing resources at things that were nice in the short term but were actually keeping them from where they wanted to go in the long term. When they began to make changes, it wasn't because they realized lattes were bad; it was because they decided a house was more important and they needed to direct their resources toward that deeper value.

To get to that place of adjusting their lifestyle, however, Mark and Faith had to come to terms with a universal reality. For every single person on the planet, from the richest to the poorest, our time, energy, and money come with *limits*. The nature of limits is that when we refuse to accept them or try to work against them, they work against us; but when we learn to work within our limits, they work for us. Before they met with me, Mark and Faith had looked at their finances and believed both that they didn't have resources for a house and that they couldn't adjust their lifestyle. They didn't see that by not limiting their spending on lattes and other small purchases, they were enforcing the larger limit of their financial power to achieve their long-term goals. When they began to work with these limits and say no in the short term, they unlocked their freedom to say yes in the long term.

But, as Mark and Faith discovered, the process of reckoning with the limits of our resources is not easy. Our relationship with our time, energy, and money is . . . well, it's complicated. Jesus said, "Where your treasure is, there will your heart be also." Our hearts are tied up in what we have in certain ways that we don't even understand until we start trying to manage our resources in a way that aligns with our God-given identity, purpose, and assignments. As we saw in the last chapter, building a long- and short-term vision for our purpose and assignments clarifies what we need to be saying yes and no to—but our yes and our no really don't happen until we point our resources toward those things. In Mark and Faith's case, it wasn't until they realized what was actually required for them to say yes to their house that they were forced to confront another competing yes in their hearts: they wanted to feel like their lifestyle matched their friends. We often don't even see how such desires are influencing and directing our decisions until we start trying to use and grow our limited resources more effectively. However, wrestling with the competing desires of our hearts and bringing them into order is how we come to master not only our resources but also ourselves so that we can truly say yes consistently to the work and the life God has entrusted to us.

Let's take a closer look at where we struggle to accept and work with the limits of our time, energy, and money; where our hearts get tangled and divided with competing desires; and how God's wisdom helps us overcome these struggles so we can become wise managers of resources who cause our lives to grow and thrive.

Time

Time is the resource that comes with the hardest limits. We all get the same twenty-four hours in a day. Sure, there are things we can do that raise the odds of us having more days to work with over a lifetime—staying physically, emotionally, and spiritually healthy; avoiding risky activities; building wealth to provide for our needs; honoring our parents (see Exodus 20:12), and more. But God alone knows what our lifespan will be. Time is also the resource that we are constantly using, whether we are aware of it or not. We can't put it in savings to use later or find some way to recharge it once it's run down. Thus, the best way to approach stewarding our time well is not trying to get more of it but maximizing the time we have. As the Bible puts it, "See then that you walk circumspectly, not as fools but as wise, *redeeming the time . . .*" (Ephesians 5:15-16, NKJV).

Maximizing our time simply means using it on what's most important. The blessing in the hard limit of time is that when we work with it productively, it forces us to clarify and give our full attention to the things that most matter when it comes to fulfilling our assignments and purpose. The down side to this hard limit is that the things that most matter turn out to be relatively few. Maximizing our time means saying no to a lot of things—to most things, in fact.

If most of us were to do an audit of the way we are using our time, similar to the exercise I did with Mark and Faith for their finances, I think we would find that a significant amount of our "disposable" time—more than we are aware of—is going to things that are not actually producing meaningful growth in our gardens. If we were then to honestly investigate why we are giving our time to these things, two main reasons would likely come to the surface. First, we're not really clear on the most important things we should be saying yes to. This makes us susceptible to saying yes to a lot of things that actually aren't that important, which is how we end up either wasting time (hello Facebook, Instagram, Netflix, and the rest of the entertainment/social media black hole) or getting busy, stressed, and overwhelmed. The second reason is that we don't want to commit to saying yes to the really important things because of what it will require us to say no to. Sometimes we don't want to say no because we feel obligated to the less important commitments to which we've bound ourselves. Sometimes we don't want to say no because we're afraid of missing out on something we want. And perhaps most often, we don't want to say no to something that is meeting our needs in the short term to focus our time on the things that only pay off in the long term.

Again, we must accept that the only way to a thriving life lies in embracing the limits of our assignments and purpose and giving them our full yes. Giving our precious time to anything else will cost us the joy, fulfillment, and success God desires us to experience. As someone who has most likely spent more of my time resources than you at this point in our lives, I can tell you that the greatest regrets in life all come from realizing you didn't spend your time on the most important things. Realizing you've wasted money and energy is frustrating, but realizing you've wasted time on things that didn't really matter is heartbreaking.

Taking careful stock of where we are spending our time and consistently pointing this resource at our calling and assignments don't just spare us from future regret; they also provide us with emotional and spiritual strength to resist the anxiety, discouragement, and frustration that often come with various experiences in the timeline of our lives. Part of our struggle with time is that we expect certain things to take so long, or for certain things to happen by a certain date. We compare ourselves with So-and-so, who wrote his first novel, released her breakthrough album, got married and had a family, started a successful business, or accomplished whatever we're trying to accomplish at a certain age, and when our lives don't match that timeline, we start to feel behind and wonder what is wrong. Or we start an important long-term project—getting in shape, writing a book, developing an innovative product, launching a startup, learning a valuable skill, saving money for a big purchase, reading through the entire Bible—and discover that it takes a lot longer than we originally thought, so we get frustrated and impatient. But when we know that we are aligned with our assignments and purpose, we can trust that even if our timeline looks different than others (of course it does—every one of our timelines is unique) and even if things are taking longer (of course they do—all good things in life take time), we don't need to worry or be discouraged, because *there is always enough time to do what God has called us to do.*

Energy

The resource of energy includes our physical strength, cognitive attention and thinking, and emotional willpower. We can think of the limits of this resource like a rechargeable battery—it can be used over a period of time and then replenished. When we work with these limits productively, we consistently practice activities that help our batteries recharge fully and sustain high levels of output. When we work against these limits, we end up burning too hot or too cold and compromise our ability to fulfill our assignments effectively.

Think back to the wise woman in Proverbs 31. This woman's capacity and output is tremendous. She is *getting things done* day after day after day, which can only mean she is *fit* for her tasks. She is physically strong and skilled, mentally focused and thinking clearly, and emotionally hopeful, joyful, and motivated. She is stewarding her energy well, and as a result, both she and everything she touches is thriving.

But fitness, whether physical, mental, or emotional, does not simply happen. If we want our bodies to achieve a certain level of mastery and perform well for us over a lifetime, we need to feed and water them well, give them regular exercise and good sleep, keep them safe, and repeatedly practice whatever skills we need them to do consistently well. The same applies to our minds and emotions—we need to give them the fuel, exercise, rest, safety, and practice in specific skills they need to operate at their highest level.

In short, stewarding our energy is really stewarding and mastering ourselves—it is practicing self-control. This is why The Message translates the fruit of "self-control" as the ability "to marshal and direct our energies wisely" (Galatians 5:23). But the very idea that self-control is a fruit indicates that it results from something happening on a higher level than our bodies, minds, and emotions. According to the Bible, our self-control, or lack of it, flows out of the central spiritual practice of our daily lives: choosing to be led by the Spirit of love and freedom, which is the only thing that produces true self-mastery, and refusing to be mastered by our own "sinful self-interest" (Galatians 5:17, MSG). The paradox is that when we don't master our bodies, minds, and emotions and give them what they need to thrive and be productive, we are being selfish; but when we do master them and maximize their output to fulfill our assignments, we are loving ourselves, God, and others, who all benefit from using our energies this way.

The daily practice of leaning into the Holy Spirit leads us to radical self-acceptance. It's the Holy Spirit who clears away all the false narratives we've heard our whole lives about who we are and makes our identity as loved sons and daughters of the Father real to us. When we learn to see ourselves through His eyes, we finally see the healing truth that *we are enough*. The assignments and purpose our Father has given us are great and important, and He has given them specifically to us because He actually designed and built us for them. As Paul wrote, "For we are God's masterpiece. He has created us anew in Christ Jesus, so we can do the good things he planned for us long ago" (Ephesians 2:10, NLT).

Radical self-acceptance frees us from every false limit that has been holding us back from our potential. It also removes every excuse that has been keeping us from taking responsibility for that potential. God has entrusted us with this body, this mind, this heart, and this life, and we owe it to Him, ourselves, and the world to steward it well.

Money

If we were to ask people what their most limited resource is, many would likely point to money or material possessions. But unlike our time and energy, which are pretty strictly limited by our physical existence and lifespan, our money is the resource that has the greatest capacity for growth. For this reason, the state of our finances is more completely determined by *our choices*, which in turn are determined by our *core values and beliefs*, than any other resource in our lives. This is one of the reasons Jesus talked so much about our relationship with money—it most clearly reveals what we truly believe about God, ourselves, and the world, and what we most value.

As someone who has talked with people about managing their personal finances for many years, I can confidently say that our greatest limits around money exist in our minds and hearts. This is partly due to lack of financial training, but it is primarily due to a belief and value system based in shame and powerlessness. Through experiences such as dealing with a lack of financial resources growing up, making poor financial choices, or falling into addictive cycles of impulse spending and debt, we come to fear money. When money causes us anxiety, stress, anger, hopelessness, or fear, then it is no longer a resource we are managing to achieve our assignments and purpose. It is not serving us; we are serving it. Whenever we serve something that we were meant to master, it produces shame and powerlessness.

Here are some of the classic signs that we are serving, rather than mastering, our money:

- We're afraid to even think or talk about money, much less ask for help learning to manage it.
- We don't look regularly at where our money is going or plan a budget.
- We spend any financial surplus we have on short-term needs or pleasures.
- We buy things we can't afford.
- We struggle to celebrate the financial success of others.
- We struggle to save, invest, or give generously.

In contrast, when we are free from the fear of money and managing it wisely, we will:

- Regularly look at the state of our finances so we know where they are going.
- Create a budget and stick to it.
- Ask for help and wisdom from others so we can learn how to use our money more effectively.
- Examine our financial decisions carefully and refrain from impulsive purchases.
- Buy only things we can afford and avoid going into debt.
- Use our surplus to save, invest, and give generously.

So how do we make the shift from serving to mastering our money? As is true with any type of change we need to make in our behavior, the most critical thing we must do is to look inside and uncover the beliefs and values driving our financial choices. Tools like Sozo—Spirit-led prayer counseling—can be particularly effective in helping us identify the lies we have believed about finances, lack, or our mistakes and hold them up to the light of truth. Only when we find out *why* building a budget feels intimidating, *why* we feel so powerless and out of control with our spending, *why* someone else's success makes us feel small or bitter, etc., will we be able to see where our thinking and values are out of alignment with what God says about us.

One truth we must all embrace as wise workers and managers of resources is the truth embedded in the parable of the talents. The wealthy man in the parable gave each of his workers a sum of money "according to his ability" (Matthew 25:15). The response of the wise workers shows us what that meant. The worker who got two talents didn't look at the worker who got five and think, *My boss doesn't trust me as much as he trusts him.* He thought, *My boss believes in me and knows exactly what I can handle right now. I'm going to get busy using this so it can grow.* At any point in our stewardship journey, we must see that our current financial resources are not telling us where we have leveled off; they are telling us what we can start to build with. Our Father has entrusted us with the financial resources we have because He knows that we are capable of managing them well.

The Underlying Issue

As you may have picked up, there's a common theme that lies at the heart of our struggles to work productively with the limits of our time, energy, and money: our trust in God. This trust is the key to the parable of the talents. The wealthy man chose to trust all of his workers with resources. However, only two of the three workers chose to trust their boss by using what he had given them. The wise workers were confident that his heart toward them was good, while the unwise worker was not, which led them to treat their resources in completely opposite ways. In the same way, God has trusted all of us with time, energy, and money because He loves us and wants to see us thrive. He gives us enough to succeed because we are enough in His eyes.

In chapter 2, we considered Brené Brown's observation that we live in a culture of scarcity—the perception that not only are there not enough opportunities and resources for everyone to thrive but also that we are not enough to deserve a thriving life. This belief in our unworthiness—shame—is what relegates us to being those fearful, self-interested, unwise workers who waste the resources of our lives on things that don't matter and sabotage our true heart's desires to do rewarding work, culti-vate healthy and nourishing relationships, and leave a meaningful legacy. But discovering that we are enough in the Father's eyes sets us free from the perception of scarcity. We can trust that we have every resource and opportunity we need to fulfill our assignments. We can trust that we can and will succeed in learning to maximize our time, achieve great energy output and fitness, and manage our finances well. And ultimately, we can trust that we will thrive in life as our Father desires.

"Someone's sitting in the shade today because someone planted a tree a long time ago."

Warren Buffett

CHAPTER 10

Trust and the Art of Planning

As you may have noticed, the issue of trust in God has come up again and again as we have explored His wisdom for how to approach our work, career, passion, relationships, balance, and resources. There's a very good reason for this.

Think back to Genesis 3, where the enemy succeeded in breaking up the partnership between humans and God and bringing all of our work, relationships, and culture-making under a curse. How did he do this? Let's look again at that ancient and timeless conversation:

> Now the serpent . . . said to the woman, "Did God really say, 'You must not eat from any tree in the garden'?" The woman said to the serpent, "We may eat fruit from the trees in the garden, but God did say, 'You must not eat fruit from the tree that is in the middle of the garden,

and you must not touch it, or you will die.'" "You will not certainly die," the serpent said to the woman. "For God knows that when you eat from it your eyes will be opened, and you will be like God, knowing good and evil." (Genesis 3:1-5, NIV)

First, the enemy put words in God's mouth He had never said. Second, he flatly contradicted the words God had actually said. Third, he accused God of lying to Adam and Eve because He wanted to withhold something good from them. All three hammered home the same message: *You cannot trust God.*

This was the lie that ruined everything. This was the lie that led the human race to abandon their apprenticeship to God and cut themselves off from His wisdom for life. This is the lie beneath all the other lies, which continues to lead generation after generation to keep trying to do life on our own terms, resulting in frustration and fruitlessness.

The good news is that Jesus breaks the power of this lie. He not only tells us the truth, but He *is* the Truth that *we can trust God*. In Jesus, we see that God the Father is not withholding anything good from us. In fact, He is giving us every good thing—especially Himself. As Paul said, "He who did not spare his own Son, but gave him up for us all—how will he not also, along with him, graciously give us all things?" (Romans 8:32). He is certainly not withholding knowledge and wisdom from us—the thing humans wanted when they took the fruit—for in Christ "are hidden all the treasures of wisdom and knowledge" (Colossians 2:3).

This was why Jesus came to Earth two thousand years ago. He didn't just come to forgive our sin and take us to heaven when we die. He came to destroy the lie that cuts us off from the life we were made for, a life of joyful partnership with God and one another, and a life of meaningful, creative work that causes us, others, and the world to flourish. He came to bring us back to a life founded on deep, unshakable trust in Him.

This is why one of my life verses is Proverbs 3:5-6: "Trust in the LORD with all your heart, And lean not on your own understanding; In all your ways acknowledge Him, And He shall direct your paths" (NKJV). I also like how the Passion Translation puts it: "Trust in the Lord completely, and do not rely on your own opinions. With all your heart rely on him to guide you, and he will lead you in every decision you make. Become intimate with him in whatever you do, and he will lead you wherever you go."

These verses make it clear that trust is not a mental exercise. It is a relational heart posture based in personal knowledge—knowledge that increases as we learn to walk with the Lord through every day, situation, and season of life. Specifically, it's a posture of *leaning* on Him. Think about what it means to lean on someone who is guiding you forward. You have to get close enough to touch them, vulnerable enough to let your weight rest on them, and willing enough to keep in step with them. That's trust.

So many believers are missing out on this *leaning* relationship of trust with Jesus. For them, the idea of working for God or being His apprentice suggests a distant boss-employee relationship, not an intimate partnership. Some, like the unwise worker who buried his talent, see the Father as hard and punishing. Many others simply find it hard to believe that God actually loves them that much—that He actually wants to walk closely with them as their loving Father and show them how to live. But that's exactly how much He loves us, and this is what our journey as sons and daughters is all about: discovering the incredible love of the Father for us as we learn to trust Him by stepping into His design for how to live.

Planning Pitfalls

Throughout this book, we've covered many aspects of what it looks like to work and build a life based on trust in God. As we've seen, the life of wise work God leads us toward as we lean on Him is a life of *purpose* and *passion*—a life where we are developing long-term vision for what we are called to do and become *and* paying the price of hard work to fulfill our present assignments. In this final chapter, I want to talk about how God instructs us to approach the art of *planning* from a posture of deep trust in Him.

The book of Proverbs refers repeatedly to the importance of planning and how we should approach it:

> Your plans will fall apart right in front of you if you fail to get good advice. But if you first seek out multiple counselors, you'll watch your plans succeed. (Proverbs 15:22, TPT)

> Go ahead and make all the plans you want, but it's the Lord who will ultimately direct your steps. (Proverbs 16:1, TPT)

> Before you do anything, put your trust totally in God and not in yourself. Then every plan you make will succeed. (Proverbs 16:3, TPT)

Within your heart you can make plans for your future,
but the Lord chooses the steps you take to get there.
(Proverbs 16:9, TPT)

Honor God's holy instructions and life will go well for
you. But if you despise his ways and choose your own
plans, you will die. (Proverbs 19:16, TPT)

A person may have many ideas concerning God's plan
for his life, but only the designs of his purpose will succeed in the end. (Proverbs 19:21, TPT)

If you solicit good advice, then your plans will succeed.
So don't charge into battle without wisdom, for wars are
won by skillful strategy. (Proverbs 20:18, TPT)

The theme that runs through these verses is that planning is good—
as long as it's anchored in trust in God and godly counsel. So what does
trust-based planning look like? Before I answer that, I want to describe
what it *doesn't* look like. In my experience and observation, there are
two problematic approaches to planning that believers often fall into
that we must avoid if we hope to experience the thriving, fruitful life
our Father desires for us.

The first of these common planning pitfalls is *under-planning*. People
who talk a lot about being "Spirit-led" often seem to have this problem.
Jesus once used the wind as a metaphor in describing those who are
born of the Spirit: "you cannot tell where it comes from or where it is
going" (John 3:8). Apparently, some people wrongly interpret this to

mean that if you're led by the Spirit, you should just drift along through life without a plan, blindly trusting God to tell you what to do and provide for your needs.

While there are certainly seasons in our walk with the Lord where He is teaching us total, moment-by-moment dependence, as He did leading the Israelites through the wilderness and feeding them with manna, this approach is not what He intends for us long term. Think again of the journey of apprenticeship. In the early years, an apprentice does have to be a pure learner who is at the beck and call of the master craftsman. He has to learn the basics, step by step, and may not understand for a long time the larger purpose or plan for the tasks he is being assigned. In *The Karate Kid*, for example, Mister Miyagi teaches Daniel to "wax on" and "wax off." For a long time, he doesn't have a clue what these fundamentals are all about. But eventually the day comes when the skills he's been practicing come together in a fighting strategy.

Believers who cling to under-planning throughout their life aren't being led by the Spirit. Ultimately, they're being irresponsible, because they never really put what God has given them to use to build something that will provide lasting benefit to others. They don't actually trust God enough to pursue their true purpose and put in the work to develop their passion. In chapter 1, I shared the story of Pastor Lewis, who retired from a forty-year career in ministry just as dependent on the charity of others at the end of his life as he had been at the beginning, and with a legacy of mediocre spiritual leadership. Sadly, Pastor Lewis represents a number of people I have known and observed in my life. Instead of reaching the end of their lives with "spoils" to share—especially the spoils of character, wisdom, and generous investment in the lives of others—they are still living in survival mode. Please hear me: I am not saying the measure of success is having a strong retirement account. However, in many cases this is just one sign of how people under-plan for their futures and fail to reach their full potential.

The other planning pitfall leads to the same place of fruitlessness, but through the opposite extreme of *over-planning*. Unlike under-planners, who have insufficient vision for their future, over-planners love to plot out their five, ten, and twenty-year plans in detail. They have Disney-vivid dreams for how their lives will turn out, which sets them up for an obvious collision course with real life, which absolutely will not happen exactly according to their expectations. This sets them up to make a couple choices: either they will get frustrated, confused, disappointed, and bitter when their real lives fall short of what they had planned or they will stubbornly cling to life in fantasy land and do all they can to ignore, escape, or avoid reality's unwelcome intrusions.

One over-planner I met was a man in his early thirties who told me he had seven businesses, with plans to start more. He described them all to me and then asked, "I'm trying to decide which business should be my umbrella corporation. What do you think?"

I asked, "Which is the most profitable?"

He stopped and looked at me, puzzled. "Well, none of them are profitable yet."

I was getting the picture that this guy had some gaps in understanding how to build a successful enterprise. I explained why I thought his best strategy was to stop starting businesses, close down most of the ones he had, pick the business that was doing the best, and pour all his energy into making it profitable.

The man was not happy with this advice. He had a dream of being an entrepreneur with multiple businesses, but his lofty plans left out many of the critical elements for actually realizing this dream, including putting in his 10,000 hours to develop an excellent product or service, mastering the core disciplines of business, and nurturing a new business to profitability. The more we spoke, the more it became evident that he didn't want to let go of his fantasy plan and accept reality.

While under-planners tend to be passive victims who let life happen to them, over-planners aggressively cling to control. But the core issue with both of them is the same: they don't really trust God enough to embrace His plan and process for their lives. As a result, they end up in the same place. At first glance, they may appear to be good-hearted, Jesus-loving people, or accomplished, successful people who got their dream job, spouse, house, or career. But when you look more closely at the fruit of their lives—not only what they've built and accomplished, but who they have become and the impact they've had on others—the façade falls away and you see the truth that they are, in fact, orphans and survivalists. They've never really stepped into their true identity as sons and daughters and embraced their apprenticeship journey with the Father.

Wise Planning and Resilience

So what does it look like to make plans from a posture of trust and leaning on the Father? As I have often emphasized in this book, people who refuse to look for shortcuts in life but embrace God's proven path to their purpose, passion, and potential cultivate *long-term vision* for fulfilling their purpose and leaving a legacy over their lifetimes, while also giving their full focus to their *present assignment*, which doesn't always look like it's connected to a larger, long-term plan. Like Chris, many of us go from assignment to assignment without really seeing how they are all connecting and coming together to help us fulfill our purpose. Sometimes these assignments seem to make no sense and even look like the exact opposite of what we feel called to do. Those who choose to trust God and lean in to Him are able to balance and live in the tension between the now and the not-yet in their personal journeys.

Joseph is the classic biblical example of someone who received a vision about his future as a young man, and then ended up in assignment after assignment that seemed the furthest thing from that vision. But finally the day came when his vision was realized, and he saw how all the work he had done managing Potiphar's estate and an Egyptian prison had prepared him to manage a nation as Pharaoh's right-hand man. The only way he ended up there was by trusting God enough to keep working, even when it looked like it would never lead to the vision.

The art of great planning grows out of being fiercely committed to God's grand, epic vision and purpose for our lives while also being fiercely committed to facing our present reality from a posture of leaning on Him. By living into the tension between these two things productively, we not only grow and accomplish what we need to accomplish, but we also develop the character quality that is arguably one of the most important qualities our Father wants to cultivate in us: *resilience*.

According to the dictionary, resilience is "the ability to recover quickly from difficulties; toughness" and "the ability of a substance or object to spring back into shape; elasticity." There's no such thing as a life without problems, challenges, difficulties, tests, and trials. We're all going to go through the wringer in some way at some point, and we will never become wise planners without taking this into account. We obviously can't plan everything that will happen in life, but what we can do is choose to train ourselves to respond to what happens in a way that enables us to bounce back, recover, and grow through difficulties, rather than being crushed by them.

In her *Harvard Business Review* article "How Resilience Works," Diane Coutu explains that there are three primary traits resilient people display in their response to difficulties and challenges. First, resilient people have "a staunch acceptance of reality."[15] Resilient people aren't optimists who candy-coat problems, ignore unpleasant possibilities, or build castles in the clouds, she explains. Rather, they have the courage to face the good, bad, and ugly in every situation.

The second trait resilient people display is "a deep belief, often buttressed by strongly held values, that life is meaningful." This connects with the principle I quoted earlier in the book that *vision gives pain a purpose*. When pain has a purpose, it changes our entire experience of pain and orients us to endure it and allow it to work on us productively, rather than run from it.

The third and final trait of resilient people Coutu describes is "an uncanny ability to improvise." Instead of being married to plans and ending up at a loss when those plans get derailed, they know how to work creatively with the resources and opportunities at hand to regroup, recover, and move forward.

One could probably write another book just on these traits and how to develop them, but I'll just make a few points about them here. First, all of these traits are conspicuously lacking in under-planners and over-planners. Both actively refuse to face the unpleasant or uncomfortable aspects of reality. Both struggle to accept and engage with God's

15 Diane Coutu, "How Resilience Works," *Harvard Business Review*, May 2002.

meaning and purpose for their lives. And both display a rigidity or inflexibility when it comes to being able to adjust, improvise, and build creative solutions to whatever problems they encounter. This is why, while both may succeed in surviving, they never really develop the true resilience that promotes growth and flourishing.

Second, all three of these traits are all ultimately found and rooted in trust in God. To put it the other way around, one of the best ways to see that we truly *do* trust God is that we are demonstrating these three traits. If we are refusing to face some uncomfortable reality, are struggling to find meaning and purpose in life, or are unable to find creative ways to make the best of our current situation, then these are dead giveaways that we are not anchoring our hearts in trust like we need to.

Last, the fact that these traits all grow out of trust in God means that we who are learning to build everything in our lives on a posture of trust have the potential to become—and should become—the most resilient people on the planet. This is really good news. As Diane Coutu found in her research, resilience is arguably the most essential trait for building thriving and fruitful lives: "More than education, more than experience, more than training, a person's level of resilience will determine who succeeds and who fails. That's true in the cancer ward, it's true in the Olympics, and it's true in the boardroom."

So how do we cultivate these traits of trust to plan wisely and build our resilience? We must develop our own personal planning *discipline*. While in many respects this discipline will look different for each one of us, according to our unique identity, purpose, and assignments, it should incorporate four key elements: rhythm, reflection, relationship, and recalibration. Let's briefly explore each of these.

Rhythm

If you have any experience gardening or working in agriculture, you know that raising plants or crops to flourish and be fruitful involves performing tasks that repeat at intervals. There are certain things you need to plan up to a year or more in advance (which crops you'll plant and when), things you need to plan on a seasonal or quarterly basis (pruning, pollinating, harvesting), things you need to plan monthly and weekly (fertilizing, watering), and things you plan on doing each day (weeding, checking on pests).

The same principle applies to our personal gardens. As we saw in chapter 8, these gardens generally incorporate at least the five following areas:

- Relationships (God, spouse, kids, friends, work colleagues, etc.)
- Personal health (physical, psychological, spiritual)
- Employment (what you do to make a living)
- Other meaningful activities (hobbies, causes, groups)
- Maintenance (chores, bills, etc.)

Each of these plots of your garden needs different things at different intervals to flourish, depending on its nature and the season it is in. Wise planning takes all of these into account. The exercise in chapter 8 is one way to discover what each area of your garden needs to flourish and be fruitful (produce good results), which gives you the information you need to start organizing your priorities and setting goals. This is what Stephen Covey calls "beginning with the end in mind."

At the start of every year, Lauren and I fly to Hawaii together and take a few days to work on the Hasson "State of the Union." This is an annual rhythm we've established to look at each area of our lives, listen to the Holy Spirit, dream about what we hope to accomplish in the coming year, and build a plan with clear goals to achieve those results. This sets us up to see what we need to plan on a quarterly basis, which in turn clarifies the rhythms we need to set on a weekly and daily basis.

Here's the reality: the plans Lauren and I make in Hawaii never happen exactly as we envision. But clarifying our priorities, setting goals, and establishing this rhythm of planning at these different intervals give us the right balance of structure and flexibility so that we can adjust to what life throws our way while continuously moving toward our shared vision of the life we are building with each other and the Lord.

Here are some questions to ask as you establish the rhythms of your planning discipline:

- Have I clarified my vision for flourishing in each area of my life?
- Have I clearly identified the things I want to be cultivating in each area—my priorities?
- Have I clearly identified the goals I want to pursue to fulfill those priorities in this season? Are they SMART (specific, measurable, achievable, relevant, time-based) goals?
- Have I broken these goals down into appropriate time intervals, from long to short—annual, quarterly, monthly, weekly, daily?
- What kind of planning rhythm do I need to have to manage the execution process, from the daily tasks to the final result?

Reflection

In my company, we have a longstanding tradition of doing a postmortem at the end of every project and the end of every year. We sit down together and take a detailed look at everything that happened—both the good and bad. Whenever we have brought someone new onto the team who isn't familiar with this practice, they get nervous, thinking that they're about to be blamed or fired for whatever didn't go well. But as they soon discover, the entire purpose for the postmortem is to learn. We want to learn from what we did well so we can repeat that on the next job, and we want to learn from what didn't go so great so we can make sure it doesn't happen again. Yes, hashing through the details of a project or year takes work and some emotional courage, but our team has come to love this process. Without fail, we emerge feeling more connected, motivated, and equipped to tackle the next project with fresh energy and better planning.

It seems almost too obvious to say, and yet it needs to be said, because so often we try to ignore it: *We can't build a wise plan for the future without learning from the past.* The biggest reason we try to ignore the past is shame. For most of us, taking an honest look at the current state of affairs in our lives, and particularly where we have fallen or are falling short, easily triggers our old fear of punishment and disconnection. This fear tells us that all we will see when we look in the mirror is proof that we are a failure, that we can't change. But this is a lie. When we reflect on our lives with the Holy Spirit, what we see is an apprentice and loved child of God who is on a journey of growth. What we see as falling short, He calls part of successful learning.

Jesus promised us that knowing the truth would set us free. This applies on so many levels. For example, as I mentioned in the last chapter, so many of the people who come to me wanting financial advice are terrified of looking at their finances. They feel powerless to set meaningful financial goals or to change their current habits. But as soon as they face the dragon of fear and shame, learn to read their financial statements, and decide to build a budget, guess what happens? They don't feel powerless anymore. In fact, they feel incredibly empowered and confident that they can actually grow in becoming a better manager of their resources and planning to achieve their goals. This is the power and freedom that come through reflection.

Here are some questions to ask as you develop the practice of reflection in your planning discipline:

- How often do I stop to evaluate the growth and results in each area of my life?
- When I reflect on my growth and results, do I look honestly at what was good and successful? Why or why not?
- When I reflect on my growth and results, do I look honestly at where I fell short? Why or why not?
- Is there any particular area of my life I am most reluctant to reflect on? Why?
- What does my reflection practice show me about what I am believing about God, myself, and my apprenticeship journey?

Relationship

Earlier, I quoted Proverbs 15:22: "Your plans will fall apart right in front of you if you fail to get good advice. But if you first seek out multiple counselors, you'll watch your plans succeed" (TPT). Wise planners don't plan alone; they seek good advice from multiple counselors. The challenge is to find those counselors. Most people, as my friend Danny Silk puts it, "surround themselves with themselves." That is, we often instinctively feel safe with people who accept us as we are and won't challenge us too much to change and grow. These people are often peers at similar stages of their life and apprenticeship. But if we want wisdom, we need to be willing to find those who are ahead of us in certain areas and will love us enough to help us do better.

A counselor who has the ability to help you grow in wisdom is someone who has built their life on trust in God, has developed the traits of resilience—acceptance of reality, belief in meaning and purpose, and the ability to improvise—and has good fruit in their life to show for it. Second, a good counselor will impart their wisdom by speaking the truth in love—truth they don't just know about but have also learned by experience. Last, the best counselors will stick with you. They may not be at your side for every step of your plan, but they care enough about investing in your life to be available to you and follow up with you in the process.

My Uncle Lew has been a counselor in my life since I was in college, and he literally helped me save my company in our seasons of greatest crisis. We most likely would have gone bankrupt if Uncle Lew hadn't stepped in to help me negotiate restructuring our financing with the bank in those crucial times. Uncle Lew is a lawyer and an expert communicator, and it was extremely educational and confidence-building to watch him in action advocating for me, showing me how to interact with people, and coaching me on how to drive good deals. People have told me that I am an effective negotiator, and I give all the credit for that to Uncle Lew. He taught me the skills that are better caught than taught:

how to read the room and use humor, self-deprecation, and empathy to build trust, rapport, and favor with those on the other side of the table.

Another wise counselor in my life was my father-in-law, Willis Hamilton. Willie was an incredibly resilient person and businessman who weathered all kinds of difficulties and setbacks in his long career. His entire manufacturing factory once burned to the ground, but he rebuilt it and went on to greater success. Willie had a reputation as a "dream killer" among some of the people who sought him for advice. He had an uncanny ability to see everything that could go wrong with a plan and ask the questions they had never thought of, and so people thought he was trying to shoot them down, when in fact, it was quite the opposite. Willie was simply trying to help people get a full picture of reality so their plan could succeed. Whenever I was working on a new plan for my company, I brought it to Willie for feedback because I wanted him to help me see reality so I could accept it and plan for it. I credit his wisdom, born of his own resilience, for helping me and my company weather storms that many other companies would not have survived.

As you develop your planning discipline, here are some questions to help you draw on the strength and wisdom of relationships:

- Who are my advisors and counselors?
- Do these people have wisdom to offer me out of their own personal experiences and good results in their lives?
- Are these people willing to speak the truth to me and help me see reality? Do they help me see what could go wrong with my plan so I can improve it? Do I want that from them?
- Am I seeking counsel consistently enough so that I can pull on the wisdom in my relationships as the plan unfolds?

Recalibration

If you've driven anywhere with a GPS, you have probably heard it say "Recalculating" when you take an unplanned turn or encounter an unplanned obstacle on your route. When you recalculate, you don't change your destination; you simply figure out the adjustments you need to make in your plan to reach it.

One of the reasons many people never become wise planners is that they fail to befriend the timeline and pace that most change and growth in our life require. They want acceleration and quick success—shortcuts. When things don't come quickly enough, or are harder than they expect, they wrongly conclude that they must have the wrong goal or plan, throw them out, and make some drastic change. But genuine, sustainable growth and fruitfulness in our lives take time—much more time than many of us expect. When we accept this, we can slow down and recognize that often we don't need to change our priorities or goals; we simply need to recalibrate our plan, usually in fairly minor or incremental ways. If we're not achieving our goal of losing ten pounds, for example, we don't recalibrate by going on a crash diet; we might pick one or two things to focus on for a week or two, like tracking nutrition or drinking more water. If we aren't feeling as connected to our spouse as we want to be, we don't need to wait to take a two-week vacation with them; we can simply recommit to a weekly date night. This type of recalibration keeps the A (achievable) in our SMART goals, which keeps us from getting overwhelmed, frustrated, and ultimately derailed from our plan.

Here are some good questions to ask as you learn to recalibrate effectively in your planning discipline:

- When I'm not seeing the growth or results I want to see on my expected pace or timeline, how do I respond?
- Do I get frustrated, give up on my goals, look for shortcuts, or try to make a drastic change to my plan?
- Can I recognize where my expectations for the pace or timeline of growth and results are unrealistic?
- If my expectations for this particular area of growth are realistic and I'm not seeing results, what are 2 to 3 achievable adjustments I can make to my plan?

Your Hope and Future

Ultimately, every aspect of our personal planning discipline must be rooted in the firm belief that God has a good plan for our lives. This is the promise of Jeremiah 29:11: "'For I know the plans I have for you,' declares the LORD, 'plans to prosper you and not to harm you, plans to give you hope and a future.'" We must also believe that God is revealing this plan to us and giving us the wisdom we need to live it out. As I said in chapter 1, wisdom is understanding God's design (or plan) for our lives and living into that design. God promises that if we ask Him for wisdom, He will give it to us: "And if anyone longs to be wise, ask God for wisdom and he will give it! He won't see your lack of wisdom as an opportunity to scold you over your failures but he will overwhelm your failures with his generous grace" (James 1:5, TPT).

My goal and prayer in our journey together, as I said at the outset of this book, was to give you the best of the wisdom I've learned throughout my life about how to work and live well. One of the things I hope you've seen on this journey is that wisdom is not merely esoteric or intellectual but intensely practical. The only way to build effective practices in our life—whether that is doing our work, nurturing our relationships, managing resources, developing a hobby, or learning to rest and recover—is to anchor them in finding your purpose, working with passion, and fulfilling your potential.

My purpose and passion in writing this book flow from my conviction that you have a great hope and a great future. You have an incredible identity and purpose. Your assignments are tailor-made to help you grow to greatness. Your sacrifice and hard work to develop your passions matter to God, to you, and the many people you will impact through your work and example. Your story is a beautiful, unique journey of covenant relationship with God and others. Your commitment to steward all God has entrusted to you and cause it to flourish is building a legacy that will nourish and touch many. You were created to build a thriving, abundant life with God and put His glory and goodness on display for the world.

There are no shortcuts to this amazing life—not because it's supposed to be hard, but because God doesn't want us to miss one moment of the journey! His promise is sure: If we trust Him and stay on His proven path to our purpose, passion, and potential, we *will* succeed.

More Resources
from Bob Hasson

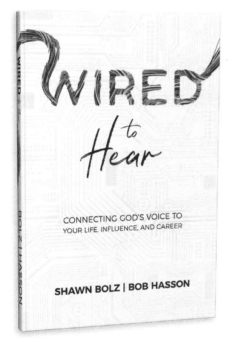

bobhasson.com